14311

D1103731

TOO MANY TOMATOES . . .

G·K
Hall
&Cº

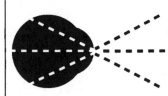

This Large Print Book carries the
Seal of Approval of N.A.V.H.

TOO MANY TOMATOES,

SQUASH, BEANS, AND OTHER GOOD THINGS

A Cookbook for When Your Garden Explodes

LOIS M. LANDAU & LAURA G. MYERS

G.K. Hall & Co.
Thorndike, Maine

Published in 1997 by arrangement with
HarperCollins Publishers, Inc.

G.K. Hall Large Print Reference Collection.

The text of this Large Print edition is unabridged.
Other aspects of the book may vary from the original edition.

Set in 16 pt. Plantin by Juanita Macdonald.

Printed in the United States on permanent paper.

Library of Congress Cataloging in Publication Data

Landau, Lois M.
    Too many tomatoes, squash, beans, and other good things:
a cookbook for when your garden explodes / Lois M. Landau
& Laura G. Myers.
        p.   cm.
    Originally published: 1st ed. New York : Harper & Row,
c1976.
    Includes index.
    ISBN 0-7838-8210-6 (lg. print : hc : alk. paper)
    1. Cookery (Vegetables)   I. Myers, Laura G.   II. Title.
TX801.L295   1997
641.6'5—dc21   97-8469

To
Bill, Lori, and Doug Burrows
Glen, Andy, and Grant Myers
for their faith, understanding, and love

ACKNOWLEDGMENTS

We would like to give special thanks to the following friends: Nan Wooldridge, Deanne Violich, Kristin Robbins, Em Nelson, Alice Brown, Marcia Bugarini, Noreen Ferris, Douglas Williams, and James B. Taylor.

L.M.B.
L.G.M.

CONTENTS

INTRODUCTION

People of all persuasions and climates are discovering the joys of vegetable gardening. The seed companies cannot keep up with the demand; metal lids for home canning are becoming collector's items. The recent backyard garden boom seems to be a surprise to all, for although it is clearly symptomatic of inflationary food prices, it has an emotional appeal as well. This appeal is probably as simple as "getting back to basics." Finding the land can work for you in this time of pollution and processed food is a refreshing and awakening experience. Americans everywhere are exploring their own backyards in some effort to participate in their own sustenance.

As zealous gardeners are expanding their knowledge of horticulture, they are yielding great quantities of delicious fresh food. Producing the harvest is important, and handling the harvest properly is then crucial. Many a gardener has lovingly raised tomatoes to find himself with a bounty of twenty or thirty tomatoes per week. Some go to friends, some go to waste, and the family finds the same dreary tomato preparation on the dinner table night after night.

The handling, preparation, and storage of garden-fresh food seems to have become obsolete information. After some years of growing our own vegetables, we began to accumulate the knowledge of handling the harvest, and pooled our efforts in search of a variety of good recipes for each home-grown delicacy. It may seem trite to point out that a can of mushroom soup and a few frozen onion rings are not fine complements for snap beans freshly plucked from the vine. These recipes are simple, honest food preparations, with an occasional indulgence in a cream sauce. They are varied and interesting, for a range of needs from hors d'oeuvre to desserts.

We have devoted a chapter to each vegetable conducive to backyard gardening. The introductory text to each chapter includes general information, a brief summary of growing requirements, calorie, carbohydrate and food value information, and detailed instructions for harvest, storage, and cooking. The basic cooking preparation is included in the introductory texts. In the recipes that follow, the list of ingredients may call for cooked vegetables, as the basic cooking instructions are not always repeated with each recipe. All of the recipes in this book are for the freshest vegetables, unless otherwise noted. Fresh vegetables always cook in less time than older, tougher ones. The quantities of vegetables required are usually listed by number, such as 6 zucchini, or by cups. Bear in mind the quantities called for are based upon prime harvest size. In many cases prime vegetables are smaller than those found at the grocery store. Commercial growers cultivate varieties for size and yield, regardless of taste.

These recipes are not intended to teach cooking. There are no involved techniques, but the reader is expected to come to this book with a general understanding of basic cooking.

The harvest, then, is the focus of this book. Once grown, when do you pick it, how do you store it, and most important, how do you cook it?

BASIC INFORMATION

For preparation of fresh vegetables, the cooking water should *always* be at a rapid boil. This literally seals in freshness and color and provides a standard measure of cooking time.

Always choose perfect vegetables for freezing. Scald for the amount of time directed when water has reached a full boil. Begin timing as soon as food is added; do not wait for water to reboil. Plunge immediately into ice water to prevent further cooking. Scalding destroys enzymes that continue to change the taste and texture of foods when frozen. Seal in good-quality plastic wrap. Always label with date and contents.

Most home-frozen vegetables should be cooked while still frozen. They are generally cooked in a small amount of boiling water until heated through. The obvious exceptions to this are frozen vegetable purées, which do not need further cooking.

Don't pick fresh vegetables and let them sit while you tend to weeds and watering. Don't enjoy them as a table decoration and then plan on eating them. The vitamin content begins to deteriorate as soon as the vegetable is plucked from the garden. Eat or refrigerate immediately.

Treatment of cutting vegetables is stated in

many ways. Ranging from large to small, the terms most used are cube, dice, chop, and mince.

The complementary herbs listed at the end of each chapter introduction are not meant to suggest that the possibilities end there. Vegetables can be married to endless complementary herbs, and those listed are among the most popular combinations.

ASPARAGUS

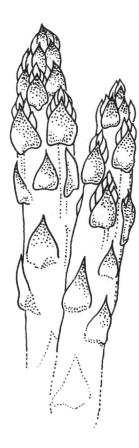

The stately asparagus is a delectable vegetable, offering something for every gardener, as it is lovely to look at, delicious, and practically self-sufficient. The lacy foliage looks much like the asparagus fern, to which it is closely related. Adaptable to any climate with spring weather, the perennial plants will produce year after year with very little effort on your part. Asparagus is one of the most economical of the vegetables to grow as well. One planting will yield annually for as long as twenty years. And it bears in early spring when nature takes care of the watering.

The French are famous for white asparagus, which is not a different plant, but merely involves a different growing technique. White asparagus is blanched by mounding the earth about 6 inches. The asparagus thus grows underground and remains white from lack of sun. When the tip protrudes, the spear is picked. White asparagus lacks vitamins and is more trouble.

The Growing The edible part of asparagus begins underground and shoots upward as a stalk or stem of the plant. The scales on the sides of an asparagus are actually the beginnings of fern leaves, and the tips of asparagus are fern leaf buds. Plants are either male or female: male plants bear more stalks, but smaller; female plants (which bear red berries in late summer) have fewer stalks, but bigger. Female stalks are considered preferable, so some gardeners make the tedious effort of weeding out the male plants and replacing them (hopefully) with female plants.

The first couple of years of asparagus culture require extra attention as well as restraint — you should not begin to harvest until the plants are 3 years old. But the responsibilities are not awesome. Plant year-old roots in early spring in a well-lined 12-inch trench to which a 4-inch layer of manure and rich topsoil has been added. Cover with about 9 inches of sandy soil. Throughout the spring and summer months gradually fill up the trench; in this manner, there is no chance of smothering the new roots. It is important to keep the bed free of deep-rooted perennial weeds. A year-round mulch is recommended by some gardeners. Yearly additions of fertilizer will increase

16

the productivity of the plants. Two 25-foot rows supply an adequate harvest for a family of four.

The Harvest The asparagus bears stalks in early spring. A choice stalk is fat and about 6 to 8 inches long. The buds at the tip should be tightly compressed. Snap off the stems rather than cutting. The portion at the bottom of the stem that is too tough to snap is too tough to eat. Low cutting may injure the stems underground before they have emerged. The harvest season is finished when the production slows down appreciably and the stems grow no longer than half an inch in diameter. Stop picking the stalks and allow them to grow into ferns, which will cause the plant to stop producing.

The Basics
1 pound = 18–24 spears = 3–4 servings.
$^2/_3$ cup cooked (3.5 ounces) = 20 calories, 3.6 grams carbohydrate, 2.2 grams protein, vitamins A and C.
Two 25-foot rows = 35 plants = 25 pounds.

The Storage Asparagus becomes tough and woody after harvest, even under refrigeration, and should be eaten within 24 hours after it is picked. Place the cut ends in water to prevent drying out, and store in the refrigerator. Or wrap in a wet paper towel and put a plastic bag over it all.

Freezing Wash. Remove scales from lower por-

17

tion with a paring knife. Start timing as soon as plunged in boiling water and scald 3 to 4 minutes, depending on the size. Chill in cold water. Drain. Package in convenient-size containers, label, and freeze.

The Cooking Asparagus is best steamed, although it may be boiled and baked. Very fresh, pencil-thin spears are good raw with a dip. Steaming may be accomplished by two means.

Basic Preparation Tie up stalks into bundles, and place bottoms down in a tall, slender pan. There should be two inches of boiling water in the bottom. Cover, reduce heat, and simmer seven minutes. Or place on a steam rack in a covered pot and steam seven minutes. Serve with butter and lemon juice or with hollandaise sauce (see p. 455).

Complementary Herbs Chives, parsley, tarragon, and thyme.

CREAM OF ASPARAGUS SOUP

2½ pounds asparagus

Boil 12 minutes or until tender; reserve 3 cups cooking liquid. Cut off tips and reserve. Cut remainder into 1-inch pieces.

¼ cup minced onion
¼ cup minced fresh parsley
1½ teaspoons ground coriander
3 tablespoons butter

Sauté until onion is soft.

2 tablespoons flour

Add and stir a few minutes.

1 chicken bouillon cube

Dissolve in reserved cooking liquid, stir into roux gradually, and simmer 5 minutes. Add stalks and purée in blender. Pour all into heavy saucepan.

½ cup heavy cream
2 tablespoons lemon juice
Salt and pepper to taste

Add to saucepan. Stir in asparagus tips.

Serves 6

Serve hot with parsley or chilled with thin slices of lemon.

ASPARAGUS WITH
SOUR CREAM SAUCE

**3 pounds asparagus,
    steamed and chilled**

Arrange on individual plates.

**1 cup sour cream
2 tablespoons grated horseradish
1 teaspoon lemon juice
   Salt and pepper to taste**

Mix and chill. Spoon over asparagus.

Serves 6

*For a colorful, cool dinner on a warm evening, serve
with chicken breasts in aspic, marinated carrots, and
sliced tomatoes.*

PIQUANT ASPARAGUS SALAD

3–4 pounds asparagus, steamed

Arrange on serving platter.

3 tablespoons tarragon vinegar
3 tablespoons cider vinegar
¾ cup salad oil
¼ teaspoon sugar
¼ cup sweet pickle relish
1 tablespoon chopped fresh parsley
1 tablespoon chopped chives

Mix together and pour over asparagus.

3 hard-boiled eggs, sliced

Decorate platter with egg slices just before serving.

Serves 8

Refreshingly different sweet-and-sour flavor. Best if marinated at least 12 hours.

ASPARAGUS MIMOSA VINAIGRETTE

1 pound asparagus

Steam 5 minutes, until crisp-tender. Chill.

$^3/_4$ cup olive oil
$^1/_3$ cup red wine vinegar
3 tablespoons Dijon mustard
Salt and freshly ground pepper

Whisk oil and vinegar until blended. Add mustard. Season to taste.

Lettuce leaves
12 mushrooms, cleaned
4 hard-boiled eggs, chilled

Arrange asparagus on lettuce. Slice mushrooms and strew over top. Grate eggs finely and mound in center. Pour dressing over.

Serves 4

A rich and delicious French dish — good as a first course.

STIR-FRIED ASPARAGUS

   2   **tablespoons oil**
   1   **clove garlic**
   1½ **pounds asparagus, sliced diagonally**

Heat oil with garlic. Remove garlic. Add asparagus. Stir over high heat until bright green, 3–5 minutes.

   1   **tablespoon cornstarch mixed with**
       ¾ cup water
       Dash of salt
   2   **teaspoons soy sauce**

Mix and pour into skillet with asparagus. Stir constantly until thick. Turn off heat. Cover until serving.

Serves 4

SPRING COLOR MEDLEY

2 cups ½-inch asparagus pieces
1 cup shelled fresh peas
1 cup sliced carrots

Parboil vegetables separately until tender-crisp.
Drain.

¼ teaspoon minced fresh tarragon
¼ teaspoon salt
Pepper to taste
3 tablespoons butter, melted
2 tablespoons chopped chives
or green onions

Add to vegetables, toss, and heat.

Serves 6

BREADED ASPARAGUS STICKS

2 pounds asparagus

Parboil 4 minutes. Drain.

1½ cups grated Parmesan cheese
1½ cups fresh bread crumbs

Mix together on a plate.

2 eggs, beaten
½ teaspoon salt
Dash of Tabasco

Mix together in shallow bowl. Dip asparagus in egg and then crumbs, coating well. Chill 20 minutes.

2 tablespoons butter
2 tablespoons olive oil

Heat in skillet. Sauté asparagus a few stalks at a time. Add more butter and oil if necessary.

Grated Parmesan cheese

Place asparagus on heated platter, sprinkle with more Parmesan cheese, and run under broiler.

Serves 6

BAKED ASPARAGUS WITH CHEESE SAUCE

1½ pounds asparagus

Steam 5 minutes. Drain.

1½ teaspoons butter
1½ teaspoons flour

Melt butter in saucepan, add flour, and cook, stirring, for several minutes.

2 cups grated Swiss or cheddar cheese
¼ teaspoon salt
¼ teaspoon prepared mustard
1½ cups milk

Add and stir until thick.

4–5 hard-boiled eggs, peeled and sliced
      Paprika or cayenne pepper

In a buttered attractive shallow baking dish, layer asparagus, eggs, sauce. Sprinkle with paprika or cayenne. Heat in 350° oven 10 to 20 minutes.

Serves 4–6

Also good if you simply pour heated sauce over asparagus and serve.

ASPARAGUS SOUFFLÉ

1 pound asparagus

Boil asparagus 5 minutes in about ½ cup water. Drain, reserving ¼ cup liquid. Cut in 1-inch pieces.

3 tablespoons butter
3 tablespoons minced green onion

Sauté until soft.

3 tablespoons flour

Stir in until blended.

³/₄ cup milk

Add along with reserved asparagus liquid, and stir until thick.

¹/₂ cup grated Swiss cheese
¹/₂ teaspoon salt
¹/₈ teaspoon pepper
Pinch of nutmeg

Add, stirring over low heat until cheese melts.

4 egg yolks

Beat a third of cheese mixture into egg yolks. Then add yolks to hot mixture. Stir well. Add asparagus.

5 egg whites, stiffly beaten
Grated Parmesan cheese

Fold whites into mixture. Place in 6-cup mold greased and dusted with cheese. Bake at 375° for 30 minutes.

Serves 4–6

ASPARAGUS CUSTARD

½ cup chopped cooked asparagus
2 eggs
1 cup light cream
¼ teaspoon salt
¼ teaspoon nutmeg
1 tablespoon butter, melted

Purée in blender.

½ cup minced cooked asparagus

Stir in. Pour into a buttered 4-cup baking dish. Place in a pan of hot water and bake at 350° about 30 minutes or until firm in center.

Serves 4

BAKED ASPARAGUS

1 pound asparagus

Arrange in gratin dish in one layer.

4 tablespoons butter
1 teaspoon sugar
½ teaspoon salt
Freshly ground pepper to taste

Dot with butter, sprinkle seasonings, and cover.
Bake at 325° for 20 minutes.

Serves 4

ASPARAGUS FRITTATA

1¹/₂ pounds asparagus

Cut into 1/2-inch pieces; place in pan with 6 tablespoons water, cover, and steam about 5 minutes until asparagus is tender and water has evaporated.

1 clove garlic, minced
1 small onion chopped
2 tablespoons oil from marinated
    artichokes, or olive oil
¹/₈-¹/₄ teaspoon dried Italian herbs

Sauté 5 minutes in large pan.

6-ounce jar marinated artichokes,
    drained and chopped (optional)
³/₄ teaspoon salt
6 eggs, beaten
¹/₂ cup milk
    Slight dash of Tabasco
¹/₂ teaspoon Worcestershire sauce

Mix together and stir in asparagus and sautéed mixture. Bake in a quiche or pie pan at 350° 15 to 20 minutes.

Serves 6

Frittatas hail from Italy. As good cold as hot, they are easy to do, high in protein and relatively low in calories, store well and can be frozen.

ASPARAGUS QUICHE

1½ cups soda cracker crumbs
6 tablespoons butter, melted

Mix and press into 9-inch pie pan.

6–7 ounces ham, slivered

Lay atop crust.

1 pound asparagus, cut into 2-inch pieces

Parboil 10 minutes. Drain and arrange over ham.

3 eggs, beaten
½ cup milk
½ cup grated Gruyère cheese
2 tablespoons onion, finely minced
½ teaspoon salt
¼ teaspoon nutmeg

Mix together. Pour over.

¼ cup grated Gruyère cheese

Sprinkle with more cheese. Bake at 350° for 25 to 30 minutes.

Serves 4

SESAME CHICKEN
WITH ASPARAGUS

1½ pounds chicken breasts

Bone and cut into 1½-inch pieces.

1½ tablespoons soy sauce
2 tablespoons sherry
1 tablespoon oil
1 clove garlic, minced
1 teaspoon finely minced fresh ginger
  (or ½ teaspoon powdered ginger)

Mix all and marinate chicken for at least 15 minutes.

½ cup cornstarch
1 cup sesame seeds
3 tablespoons oil

Stir chicken in cornstarch and then roll in sesame seeds. Cook in oil, 3 minutes per side. Remove and set aside.

1 pound asparagus

Cut diagonally into 1-inch pieces and sauté in oil. Add 3 tablespoons water, cover, and steam 3 to 5 minutes, until tender-crisp.

1 tablespoon cornstarch
1 chicken bouillon cube
1½ cups milk
2 tablespoons butter

Dissolve cornstarch and crush bouillon in milk, add butter and heat, stirring, until thickened.

Toasted sesame seeds

Place chicken and asparagus in a serving dish. Top with sauce and sprinkle with toasted sesame seeds.

Serves 4–6

An Oriental stir-fry, sesame chicken is a delectable entrée. Fresh ginger may be stored almost indefinitely in the freezer.

BEANS

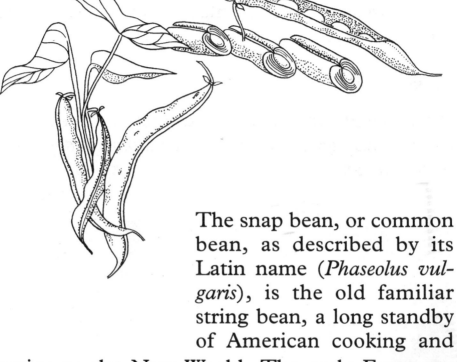

The snap bean, or common bean, as described by its Latin name (*Phaseolus vulgaris*), is the old familiar string bean, a long standby of American cooking and native to the New World. The early European explorers documented their first sight of beans being cultivated by the Indians. Since the first days of Indian farming, the common bean has seen some changes. It is no longer called string bean, since botanists have developed some varieties to a stringless state. The "snap" now refers to the very crisp state of the beans, which should snap when bent.

Although the generic label "beans" includes all the shell, bush, and climbing beans, snap beans picked when not quite full grown are the home crop for fresh cooking. Snap beans are cultivated for their tasty pod. If you allow them to stay on the vine until the beans within are easily discernible, you have fresh shell beans. Dried beans are left on the vine until the pods are almost dry — a good way to use up excess beans at the end of summer.

There are three basic varieties of snap beans: the green bean, the yellow or wax bean, and the purple bean (which turns green when cooked). You can grow pole beans, which produce a climbing vine, or compact bush beans. Kentucky Wonder pole beans have long been the gardener's favorite for their yield, cooking excellence, and use as dried beans. For a special children's treat or cocktail conversation, try the yard-long green beans known as Chinese long beans.

The Growing Snap beans need a warm temperature to germinate. Pole beans, which are ready to pick 60 to 70 days after planting, are more susceptible to cold weather, but they vastly outproduce the bush plants. Green bush snap beans can be harvested in about 50 days. Pole plants are traditionally grown with rough poles as climbing support, but they will climb a string, and an easy system is to suspend strings from an overhead string or pole horizontal to the bean row. This creates a lattice effect and facilitates harvest. Use very heavy string or nylon. Pole beans can also climb corn stalks, although the harvesting is more difficult. Plant bush beans 1 inch deep and 2 inches apart. The rows should be 2 feet apart. Be sure to plant the seeds directly in the ground, as seedlings do not transplant well. When seedlings reach 1 inch, thin to 2 plants per foot. A mid-spring planting should produce all summer.

The Harvest The bean plant has blooms like tiny sweet-pea blossoms. A snap bean is best harvested in its immature stage, when it is less than 6 inches long, before the seeds, or beans, within develop. The pods should be moist and tender, and snap when bent. Harvest beans frequently; if they are allowed to mature, the production of new pods will slow down considerably.

The Basics
1 pound beans = 3 cups (3.5 ounces) sliced = 4 servings.
1 cup cooked = 31 calories, 6.8 grams carbohydrates, 1.98 grams protein, vitamins A, B, and C.
10-foot row pole beans = about 30 pounds.
10-foot row bush beans = 10 pounds.

The Storage Refrigerate immediately. A loss of time from garden to refrigerator means a loss of taste and food value. Store the unwashed beans in a plastic sack no longer than 4 or 5 days; after that they will wilt and toughen.

Freezing Pick young crisp beans. Rinse, then snap off the tips. Beans may be frozen whole or in pieces, but do not hesitate at any point in the process. Rush from the garden and into the scalding process to prevent loss of freshness. Scald the beans 3½ minutes from the time they are put in boiling water, drain, and plunge in ice water. Drain again. Package in plastic bags of convenient size, label, and freeze.

The Cooking Beans may be cooked whole or cut into pieces, into long thin slices French-style, or into long slanting slices as the Chinese do.

Basic Preparation Wash beans. Snap off tips. Boil whole beans in small amount of salted water for 7 minutes. Serve with butter. Season to taste.

Complementary Herbs Garlic, oregano, parsley, rosemary, savory and thyme.

HERBED SNAP BEAN SALAD

4 cups sliced cooked snap beans
1 medium red onion, thinly sliced
$1/2$ cup diced green pepper
$1/2$ cup diced celery

Put all in a large bowl.

$1/8$ teaspoon dried oregano
$1/8$ teaspoon dried dill weed
$1/2$ teaspoon salt
$1/4$ teaspoon pepper
1 clove garlic, minced
$1/3$ cup oil
$1/4$ cup vinegar
$1/4$ cup red wine
$1/4$ cup sugar

Shake together in a jar and pour over salad. Cover and chill 2 to 24 hours.

Serves 6

Bean salads are always better the next day!

SESAME OIL GREEN BEAN SALAD

1 pound snap beans

Boil 5 minutes. Run under cold water.

$^1/_8$ **teaspoon salt**
2 teaspoons sugar
3 tablespoons soy sauce
1 teaspoon sesame oil

Toss with beans. Marinate 1 hour in a bowl that has been rubbed with garlic. Serve *slightly* chilled or at room temperature.

Cut clove of garlic

Serves 4

To present Chinese style, lay beans neatly all in one direction (no lettuce) on individual salad plates.

DELICATESSEN SNAP
BEAN SALAD

3 cups sliced cooked snap beans
1 onion, chopped
3 tablespoons olive oil
2 teaspoons vinegar
4 small summer squash, sliced and
     steamed 3 minutes
1 cup cooked garbanzo beans

Toss together and chill.

2½ tablespoons red wine vinegar
½ teaspoon lemon juice
1 teaspoon salt
1 teaspoon sugar
1 teaspoon dry mustard
¼ teaspoon paprika

Mix with vegetables and marinate at least overnight in refrigerator.

1 cup sour cream

Add and serve.

Serves 8

COLD GREEN BEAN MUSTARD

1 pound green beans

Boil beans 5 minutes. Run under cold water.

6 tablespoons olive oil
1 tablespoon Dijon mustard
2 tablespoons red wine vinegar
3 teaspoons chopped shallots
Salt and pepper

Whisk oil and mustard until blended. Add vinegar, shallots, and seasonings to taste.

Lettuce leaves
Minced fresh parsley

Arrange lettuce on platter, place beans on top, and pour dressing over. Sprinkle with parsley.

Serves 4

SAUTÉED SNAP BEANS

¼ **cup olive oil**
4 **cups diagonally cut snap beans**
1 **onion, minced**
4 **cloves garlic, minced**
1 **green pepper, minced**
½ **cup minced celery**

Sauté 5 minutes.

¼ **cup white wine**
½ **teaspoon sugar**

Add, cover and simmer until beans are tender-crisp.

3 **tablespoons chopped fresh parsley**
1 **tablespoon capers**
1 **hard-boiled egg, cut into eighths**

Transfer beans to serving plate and garnish.

Serves 6

This is also delicious served cold.

GRANDMA'S GREEN BEANS

6 slices bacon, chopped
2 onions, sliced

Sauté bacon and onions in large saucepan until bacon is crisp.

1 pound snap beans
Salt and pepper to taste

Add beans, season, cover with water, and simmer covered for 2 hours.

2 tablespoons sugar

Add and simmer 30 more minutes.

Serves 4–6

Cooked long and slowly, the beans are soft yet chewy. This Southern technique may upset nutritionists and French gourmets, but it's a surefire way to make folks love you.

GREEN BEANS WITH MARINARA SAUCE

1 tablespoon butter
1 tablespoon olive oil
1 large clove garlic, minced
5 sprigs fresh parsley, chopped

Sauté 5 minutes in large skillet.

$1/_8$ teaspoon salt
$1/_4$ teaspoon pepper
6 ripe tomatoes, peeled, seeded, and diced, or 1-pound can plum tomatoes, drained and chopped
1 teaspoon dried oregano

Add to skillet. Simmer 30 minutes.

1 tablespoon tomato paste, or 3 tablespoons tomato sauce
1 teaspoon anchovy paste (optional)

Stir in and remove from heat. Check seasonings.

6 cups sliced cooked snap beans

Heat beans and pour sauce over. May be reheated in oven.

Serves 6–8

SWEET-AND-SOUR GREEN BEANS

2 eggs, beaten
2 tablespoons vinegar
4 tablespoons water
1½ tablespoons sugar
½ teaspoon dry mustard
¼ teaspoon salt

Mix well in saucepan. Simmer, stirring constantly, until thickened.

4 cups cut cooked snap beans

Mix into sauce and heat gently.

Serves 4–6

SNAP BEAN FRITTERS

**3–4 cups uniformly sliced snap beans,
cut into ¼- to 1-inch pieces**

Boil 7 minutes. Drain well.

**1½ cups flour
3 teaspoons baking powder
1 teaspoon salt
1 cup finely grated Parmesan cheese
1 egg, beaten
1 cup milk**

Mix well. Stir in beans.

Oil for deep frying

Drop batter by tablespoonfuls into hot oil. Fry 3
to 4 minutes, turning once. Drain on paper towels.

Serves 6

*For an appetizer, cook ahead, reheat, then serve with
freshly grated Parmesan cheese as a dip. Use green
or yellow beans or a combination.*

SWISS BEANS

6 cups French-cut green beans

Parboil 3 minutes. Drain and arrange in shallow casserole.

2 tablespoons butter
2 tablespoons flour

Melt butter, stir in flour, and cook, stirring, for several minutes.

¾ teaspoon salt
¼ teaspoon pepper
1 teaspoon sugar
3 tablespoons minced onion

Add and stir over medium heat to blend.

1 cup sour cream

Stir in. Pour sauce over beans.

½ pound Swiss cheese, grated

Sprinkle atop. Bake in 350° oven for 30 minutes.

Serves 6–8

Very hearty and full of protein.

SNAP BEAN SUPPER

  3 **tablespoons butter**
  1 **medium onion, chopped**
  3 **stalks celery, sliced**

Sauté until soft.

  3 **tablespoons flour**

Stir in. Cook over low heat.

1½–2 **cups cubed ham**
  3 **cups sliced snap beans, cooked**
  1 **cup grated cheddar cheese**
  ½ **cup beef broth**
    Salt and pepper to taste
  ¼ **teaspoon dried thyme**

Mix all well with above. Pour into casserole.

    Bread crumbs
  2 **tablespoons butter**

Sprinkle on bread crumbs. Dot with butter. Bake covered 30 minutes at 350°. Uncover and slide under broiler to brown top.

Serves 4

DILLY BEANS

　2　**pounds snap beans**
　2　**quarts boiling water**
　1　**tablespoon salt**

Boil uncovered 5 minutes or until tender-crisp. Plunge into cold water. Drain.

　2　**teaspoons mustard seed**
　2　**teaspoons dried dill weed**
　1　**teaspoon crushed hot chili peppers**
　1　**teaspoon dill seed**
　4　**cloves garlic, whole**
　2　**cups water**
　2　**cups white vinegar**
　$^2/_3$　**cup sugar**
　2　**tablespoons salt**

Bring to a boil. Pour over beans. Cool and cover. May be divided into jars for storage. Keep refrigerated.

4 quarts

BEETS

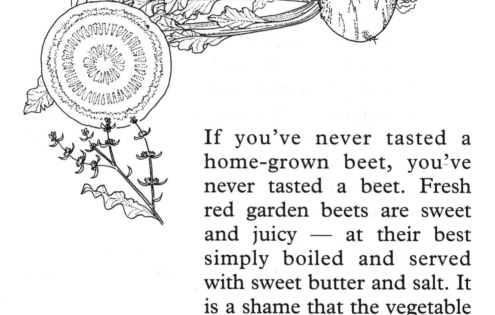

If you've never tasted a home-grown beet, you've never tasted a beet. Fresh red garden beets are sweet and juicy — at their best simply boiled and served with sweet butter and salt. It is a shame that the vegetable deteriorates so pronouncedly into the tough, bland beet we find at the grocery store.

Beets are among the most versatile growers of the vegetables, as they offer both the root and the green leaves. The "beet" itself is the root, and for this reason beets are called a root crop. All beet greens, however, are edible and extremely nutritious, though only the young leaves are much good. Pick a few leaves when the plant is young, leaving enough to feed the beet below. Cook the beet greens like chard.

The Growing Beets are a cold-weather crop, but tolerant of heat. They can withstand temperature ranges of 30° to 80°. When the weather gets too hot for them they get tough and lose sweetness. Beets will not grow in acid soil. Wood ashes and lime may be added to correct this problem.

Plant seeds in rows spaced 12 inches apart, scattering seeds at ½-inch intervals and ½-inch deep. The seed is a fruit containing two to six kernels, so the plants come up in clumps. Thin plants 3 inches apart when they are 1½ inches tall. *Be sure to save the thinnings for the dinner salad,* unless you want to use them for transplanting. Seeds vary by maturation date and type. They mature anywhere from 55 to 80 days. The longer-maturing varieties, called winter or late beets, can be stored in the ground until freezing weather. Plant in early spring and be sure to plan for successive crops to avoid too many beets at once.

The Harvest Most beets are red, but there are also yellow and white varieties. Beets are round or spindle-shaped. The round ones should not be allowed to exceed 3 inches. Baby beets, 1½ to 2 inches, are a great delicacy. Pull beet from the ground at the base of greens.

The Basics

1 pound = six 2-inch beets = 1½ cups cut = 4 servings.

½ cup cooked beets (3.5 ounces) = 40 calories, 6 grams carbohydrates, 0.9 grams protein, fairly low in vitamins and minerals when compared with the greens.

½ cup raw greens = 24 calories, 4.6 grams carbohydrates, 2.2 grams protein, high in minerals and vitamins, especially vitamin A.

10-foot row = 15 to 20 pounds.

The Storage Cut off tops 2 inches above crown. Store in a plastic bag for several days.

Freezing Freeze only mature beets. The young ones are too valuable for the freezer. Cut off tops 2 inches above crown. Cover with cold salted water. Boil 30 minutes. Slide skin off and cut off crown and root. Slice or dice. Package in bags of convenient size. Label.

The Cooking Simply cut tops 2 inches above crown and wash beets. If the crown or taproot is cut, the beet will bleed when cooked.

Basic Preparation Cover mature beets with cold salted water. Boil 30 minutes to 1 hour. Cool. Slide off skin and cut crown and taproots. Serve with sweet butter and salt. For baby beets, boil only 20 minutes, or scrape off skin, cut crown and taproot, shred, and simmer in very small amount of salted water 8 minutes. For beet greens, cook well-washed leaves in a covered pan with a small amount of boiling water for 3 to 5 minutes. Drain and season.

Complementary Herbs Basil, chives, dill, parsley.

BEET BORSCHT

4 medium beets, peeled

Cook in water to cover 20 to 30 minutes until tender. Reserve 1 cup liquid. Dice beets.

¼ cup minced Bermuda onion
1½ cups minced cucumber
4 cups buttermilk
1 teaspoon salt
½ teaspoon Worcestershire sauce

Combine with diced beets and reserved liquid and chill at least 4 hours.

Serves 6

Be sure to peel beets before cooking to make sure all dirt is removed. Otherwise liquid may have a gritty residue.

SHREDDED RAW BEET SALAD

2 cups coarsely shredded raw beets
1/4 cup vinegar
1/3 cup oil
  Salt and pepper to taste
  Juice of 1/2 lemon

Mix and chill at least 30 minutes.

3 cups shredded lettuce
1 tablespoon chopped chives
1-2 shredded carrots (optional)

Add, toss, and serve.

Serves 6

Almost calorieless, but with the zing and appeal of something more prohibitive.

TANGY BEET SALAD

1 cup hot beet liquid
3-ounce package lemon gelatin

Stir until gelatin dissolves.

$^2/_3$ cup orange juice
2 tablespoons vinegar
1 teaspoon salt
2 teaspoons grated onion
1 tablespoon grated horseradish

Add and stir to mix. Chill until syrupy.

1 cup minced celery
2 cups cooked minced beets

Stir in. Pour into individual molds and chill.

Serves 8

SWEET-AND-SOUR SHREDDED BEET SALAD

3 cups shredded cooked beets
2 tablespoons lemon juice
2 teaspoons grated lemon peel

Toss together.

2 tablespoons vinegar
2 tablespoons brown sugar
¼ teaspoon salt

Simmer to boiling. Pour over beets and chill.

Serves 4

Spoon beets over lettuce leaves on salad plates and top with thinly sliced onion.

HARVARD BEETS

½ **cup sugar**
½ **tablespoon cornstarch**
¼ **cup vinegar**
¼ **cup water**
2 **tablespoons oil**

Stir together in saucepan in order given. Boil 5 minutes.

6 **medium beets, cooked and sliced**

Stir in. Simmer 20 minutes.

Serves 4–6

ORANGE BEETS

6 raw medium beets, peeled and sliced
3 tablespoons bread crumbs
¼ cup sugar

Layer in buttered casserole.

1 tablespoon lemon juice
½ cup orange juice

Pour over beets. Cover and bake 1 hour at 350°.

Buttered bread crumbs

Sprinkle crumbs atop and run under broiler.

Serves 4

BEETS IN HORSERADISH SAUCE

6 medium beets

Cook and skin. Slice.

¾ cup water
1 tablespoon cornstarch
¼ teaspoon dry mustard
¼ cup sugar
2 tablespoons vinegar
2 tablespoons grated horseradish
1 tablespoon butter

Cook until thickened. Add sliced beets. Cook to color sauce.

Serves 4

PICKLED BEETS AND EGGS

½ teaspoon ground cloves
1½ teaspoons celery seed
1½ teaspoons cinnamon stick
1 cup sugar
1 cup vinegar
1 cup water
½ teaspoon salt

Tie spices into bag. Boil all a few minutes.

10 small beets, cooked and peeled
5 hard-boiled eggs, peeled

Pour hot liquid over beets and eggs. Cool and refrigerate.

6 cups

The pickled eggs must be used fairly soon, but the beets can be refrigerated for 2 weeks.

BEET AND ONION PICKLES

24–30 small beets, cooked and peeled
6 medium onions, peeled

Cut in quarters or slices.

5 cups vinegar
5 cups sugar
1½ tablespoons mustard seed
1 tablespoon celery seed
1 tablespoon dill seed
½ teaspoon salt
2 teaspoons turmeric

Mix in large kettle. Bring to boil. Reduce heat and cook 15 minutes. Pour over beets. Chill.

5 pints

BROCCOLI

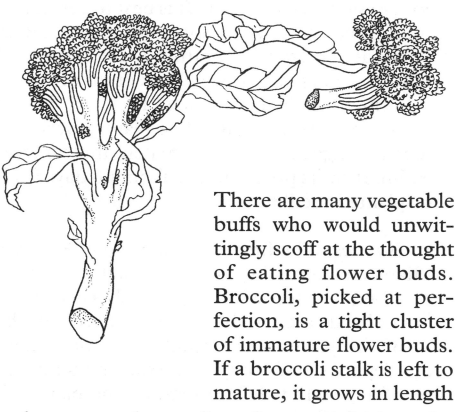

There are many vegetable buffs who would unwittingly scoff at the thought of eating flower buds. Broccoli, picked at perfection, is a tight cluster of immature flower buds. If a broccoli stalk is left to mature, it grows in length and opens to lacy yellow flowers (which make nice arrangements). Sprouting, or Italian, broccoli is a member of the cole family, all descendants of the wild European cabbage. It is most closely related to cauliflower, although its cooking uses are more like asparagus. (Most broccoli and asparagus recipes are interchangeable.) Broccoli cuisine seems to have originated in southern Italy or Sicily, as indicated by its Latin name, *Brassica oleracea italica.*

The Growing Broccoli prefers cool temperatures, 40° to 70°, but it is not temperamental and can tolerate more heat if partially shaded. It will take light frost but not a hard freeze. Broccoli seeds are slow to germinate. It is best to germinate seeds in peat pots in a sunny window. Growth may be accelerated by putting a clear sheet of plastic over the pots. Move plants outdoors when 5 to 6 inches tall; place them 15 to 18 inches apart in rows 3 feet apart. The plant grows 2 to 4 feet in height and approximately the same in breadth. It starts producing in about 60 days from transplanted seedlings.

The Harvest The first head, about 6 to 8 inches in diameter, forms on top of the stalk in a dark green bed cluster with a purplish cast. Subsequent heads are much smaller and grow in the axis of the leaves. The number of subsequent crops depends on fertility of the soil and temperature. If any stalk is left to mature, the plant will go to seed. Some broccoli plants produce for three months. Harvest broccoli before the flowerets begin to separate just prior to opening. Don't worry, however, if one or two of the buds have begun to open. This will not affect the taste.

The Basics
1 pound = 2 three-inch heads = 4 cups flowerets = 4 servings.
²/₃ cup cooked (3.5 ounces) = 26 calories, 4.5 grams carbohydrates, 3.1 grams protein, half the

recommended daily vitamin A, three times the recommended daily vitamin C.
10-foot row = 5 plants = 20 heads of assorted sizes.

The Storage It is not necessary to wash broccoli before refrigeration. Store it in plastic bags in the refrigerator. It will keep 4 to 5 days; after that it wilts and toughens and the buds begin to open.

Freezing Remove leaves and trim bottom stalks. Slice lengthwise to make equal-sized pieces so the scalding process will be uniform. Soak 30 minutes in cold salty water. Steam 5 minutes, plunge into ice water, and drain. Pack the broccoli tightly in plastic sacks of convenient size, label, and freeze.

The Cooking Don't ever peel garden-fresh stems! They will stay tender up to 5 days and contain much of the food value. You may make lengthwise slashes in very thick stalks to hasten cooking. Before cooking broccoli, soak it 30 minutes in cold salty water to crisp it and drive out insects.

Basic Preparation Steam 5 to 10 minutes depending on size. Serve with lemon butter (p. 453).

Complementary Herbs Caraway, chervil, dill weed, garlic, oregano, and rosemary.

BROCCOLI GUACAMOLE

1	cup chopped cooked broccoli
¼	cup sour cream
¼	cup mayonnaise
2	tablespoons grated Parmesan cheese
¼	cup grated cheddar cheese
1	teaspoon minced green onion
¼–½	teaspoon curry powder
¼	teaspoon salt
	Squeeze of lemon juice

Purée in blender. Chill.

Serves 6

Serve with corn chips and/or assorted vegetables.

CURRIED BROCCOLI
HORS D'OEUVRE

4 cups broccoli flowerets
1½ inches long

Cover with boiling water and simmer covered 5 to 7 minutes until bright green, but *not* tender. Quickly run cold water over, drain, and refrigerate.

1 cup sour cream
1 teaspoon curry powder (or less)
½ teaspoon salt
1 tablespoon prepared mustard

Mix well and refrigerate to blend flavors. Serve in bowl or on top of broccoli.

Serves 6

Broccoli spears and tomato wedges or other colorful vegetables topped with curry sauce can make this into a super salad.

BROCCOLI TARTS

  1 cup cooked broccoli

Chop.

  ¼ pound Swiss cheese, shredded
  3 green onions, minced
  1 cup light cream
  3 eggs, beaten
  1 teaspoon salt

Mix well, and then add broccoli.

  1 stick soft butter
  3 ounces soft cream cheese
  1 cup flour

Blend together butter and cheese. Add flour and mix well. Roll into balls the size of walnuts. Press into very lightly greased gem-sized muffin tins to form shells. Fill shells to the top with broccoli mixture. Bake at 400° about 20 minutes until golden. Cool about 10 minutes, then turn out. Serve hot.

2½ dozen

An interesting hors d'oeuvre. The tart shells can be refrigerated or frozen and reheated when needed. Frozen broccoli can be used; cook it just to thaw. Do not overcook. For quiche, use the same filling in an unbaked pie crust. Cook 30 to 40 minutes on lower rack of 400° oven.

SWEET-SOUR MARINATED BROCCOLI

4 cups broccoli spears, raw or parboiled and drained

Arrange in shallow dish.

$^1/_2$–1 Bermuda onion, minced
1 cup cider vinegar
$^2/_3$ cup sugar
$^1/_3$ cup salad oil
1 teaspoon salt
1 teaspoon pepper

Heat to dissolve sugar. Pour over broccoli. Cover and refrigerate at least 4 hours.

Serves 6–8

STIR-FRIED BROCCOLI

4 cups broccoli, cut in thin diagonal
   slices
1 cup sliced mushrooms
2 tablespoons peanut oil

Sauté 4 minutes, stirring constantly.

2 tablespoons soy sauce
½ teaspoon grated fresh ginger

Stir in. Cover and simmer 4 minutes.

Serves 6

The broccoli side shoots are excellent for this Chinese cooking technique. Toss in sliced ham for an easy, cheap dinner.

BROCCOLI WITH ORANGE SAUCE

3 cups broccoli
1 tablespoon oil

Sauté, stirring constantly, about 3 minutes. Pour in about $1/2$ inch of water. Cover and steam about 4 to 6 minutes, until tender-crisp. Drain and keep hot.

2 tablespoons butter
2 tablespoons flour

Melt butter, add flour, and cook, stirring constantly, for several minutes.

1 cup orange juice
1 tablespoon butter
1–2 tablespoons sugar
$1/8$ teaspoon salt
$1/8$ teaspoon cinnamon
$1/8$ teaspoon dry mustard

Add to roux and stir until thickened. Can be made early and reheated. Ladle sauce over broccoli.

Serves 4

This Mexican recipe is excellent for second- and third-crop broccoli. It can be made ahead and reheated in the oven.

71

BROCCOLI WITH PROSCIUTTO

3 cups broccoli

Steam 5 minutes.

4 tablespoons butter
2 teaspoons olive oil
3 cloves garlic

Sauté. Remove garlic.

8 slices prosciutto
Salt (optional)

Sauté prosciutto in same pan. Add broccoli. Sauté 5 minutes. Salt, if necessary.

Serves 4

BROCCOLI SOUFFLÉ

4 cubs chopped broccoli
1 small clove garlic

Parboil 7 minutes. Drain. Remove garlic.

2 tablespoons butter
2 tablespoons flour

Melt butter, add flour, and cook, stirring constantly for several minutes.

1 cup milk or cream
1 tablespoon grated Parmesan cheese
$1/_4$ teaspoon salt
$1/_8$ teaspoon pepper

Add to roux and stir until thickened.

4 egg yolks

Add a third of the sauce to the egg yolks. Then add yolks slowly to sauce, stirring constantly. Add broccoli.

5 egg whites, stiffly beaten

Gently stir $1/_3$ cup beaten whites into sauce, then fold in rest. Pour ingredients into greased and floured soufflé dish. Place in pan of hot water and bake at 350° for 30 to 40 minutes, until set.

Serves 6

TURKEY MORNAY

3 cups broccoli

Parboil 5 minutes. Drain.

2½ cups cooked turkey

Layer with broccoli in buttered casserole.

¼ cup butter
¼ cup flour
1 cup chicken broth
½ cup light cream
½ cup sauterne
Dash of Worcestershire sauce
Salt and pepper to taste

Heat together in order given. Stir until smooth and thickened. Pour over casserole.

½ cup grated Parmesan cheese

Sprinkle atop casserole. Bake at 400° for 20 minutes.

Serves 4

Broccoli and turkey season go hand in hand. This is fine for a group buffet, and the price is right when the broccoli is home grown.

BAKED BROCCOLI AND CHEESE

3–4 cups broccoli, trimmed

Parboil 7 minutes, drain, and place in buttered casserole.

2 eggs, beaten
1 cup cottage cheese
2 teaspoons minced green onion
½ teaspoon Worcestershire sauce
Salt and pepper to taste
¼ cup grated cheddar cheese

Mix and pour over broccoli.

4 tablespoons fresh bread crumbs
¼ cup grated cheddar cheese
4 tablespoons butter

Cover with cheese and crumbs and dot with butter. Bake at 350° for 20 to 30 minutes.

Serves 4–6

Almost a meal in itself nutritionally. This may be the entrée accompanied by a good fruit salad and warm yeast rolls.

BROCCOLI SPOON BREAD
WITH PARMESAN SAUCE

3 cups 2-inch broccoli pieces

Parboil 5 minutes. Drain, reserving $1/2$ cup liquid. Put broccoli in buttered 2-quart soufflé dish.

$1/2$ cup yellow cornmeal
$1^1/2$ cups milk

Cook over medium heat 5 minutes until thickened. Cool slightly.

2 egg yolks, beaten
2 teaspoons baking powder
1 teaspoon salt
1 tablespoon sugar

Stir into cornmeal mixture.

2 egg whites, stiffly beaten

Fold into batter. Pour batter over broccoli. Place dish in pan containing 1 inch of warm water. Bake at 375° for 40 to 45 minutes, until golden.

2 tablespoons butter
1 tablespoon cornstarch

Blend over low heat in saucepan.

1 cup milk
1 cup grated Parmesan cheese
$1/2$ teaspoon salt
$1/8$ teaspoon pepper
$1/4$ teaspoon nutmeg

Add to saucepan along with reserved broccoli liquid, and stir until blended and thickened. Serve with spoon bread.

Serves 6

BRUSSELS SPROUTS

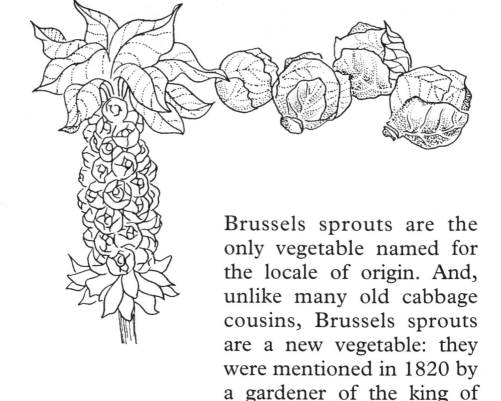

Brussels sprouts are the only vegetable named for the locale of origin. And, unlike many old cabbage cousins, Brussels sprouts are a new vegetable: they were mentioned in 1820 by a gardener of the king of Belgium, whose palace was near Brussels. This plant has an unmanicured appearance, and it seems odd to give it the name of such an elegant city. Brussels sprouts grow to a spindly height of 2½ feet. Tiny cabbagelike balls sprout at the axils of the lower leaves, and subsequent sprouts develop upward on the stalk. As the lower sprouts are harvested, and the lower leaves yellow, the plant begins to look rangy.

The Growing Brussels sprouts love cold weather. They will continue to bear when the temperature drops below 32°, and do well at as low as 20°. The tastiest sprouts grow at temperatures around 32°. As hardy as they are to freezing temperatures, it is no surprise they won't yield when it warms up. An average daily temperature of 65° is the limit. Time the planting with care. It takes 4 months from seed to beginning of harvest, 60 to 70 days from transplanted seedlings. The plant will bear over a period of 1½ months. If the weather does get too cold (or hot), uproot the plant, keep it in a garage or place with controlled temperatures, and the sprouts near maturity will develop. And, as with all cabbage relatives, do not plant where a cabbage family plant grew last year, as they are all subject to the same pests and diseases. The seeds are slow to germinate, particularly in the cool weather the plant requires for excellent harvest. Germinate them in peat pots indoors. Transplant when 6 inches tall at 1½ foot intervals. Space rows 3 feet apart.

The Harvest A Brussels sprout looks like a cabbage in miniature. It should be no larger than 2 inches and no less than 1 inch. The tiny sprouts have a flavor similar to commercial ones, but it is a greatly refined version of the same taste. (Commercial sprouts are usually too big and have a strong cabbage flavor.) Sprouts should be compact and bright green. Pick the mature ones from the bottom up. It is helpful but not necessary to pull off the leaves as they yellow, to allow the sprouts more room to grow. Always leave a crown of leaves to provide food for the plant.

The Basics
1 pound Brussels sprouts = 40 sprouts = 3½ cups = 4 servings.
⅔ cup cooked (3.5 ounces) = 36 calories = 6.4 grams carbohydrates, 4.2 grams protein, twice recommended daily vitamin C.
4 plants = 200–400 sprouts.

The Storage Store in a plastic sack in the refrigerator. It is not necessary to wash first. They will keep 3 days nicely, but are superior if cooked immediately. Don't serve a sprout hater anything but freshly harvested Brussels sprouts.

Freezing Peel outer leaves. Soak 30 minutes in salted cold water to drive out insects. Cut a shallow X in the bottom to hasten and even the cooking process. Scald 4 minutes (5 minutes if they are the full 2 inches) from the time they are plunged in boiling water. Chill in cold water. Drain, pack in bags of convenient size, label, and freeze.

The Cooking Soak 30 minutes, then cook in water or sauté. Brussels sprouts should be parboiled before being used in a casserole.

Basic Preparation Peel outer leaves. Cut a shallow X in the bottom of larger ones to even the cooking. Cook in 2 inches of boiling water 7 minutes. Drain. Season. Serve with butter. Very small sprouts may be sautéed in a covered skillet about 20 minutes.

Complementary Herbs Cloves, garlic, ginger, nutmeg.

MARINATED BRUSSELS SPROUTS

4 cups Brussels sprouts, cooked

Drain and place in bowl.

½ cup tarragon vinegar
½ cup oil
1 small clove garlic, minced
1 tablespoon sugar
1 teaspoon salt
Dash of Tabasco
2 tablespoons sliced green onion

Mix and pour over sprouts. Chill.

Serves 6

Serve with toothpicks for hors d'oeuvre, or nested in lettuce cups for salad. The smallest sprouts are suitable for this.

BRUSSELS SPROUT FRITTERS

    4 cups Brussels sprouts

Parboil 5 minutes, drain, and chop.

  1½ cups flour
    1 cup grated Parmesan cheese
    2 eggs, beaten
   ¾ cup light cream
    3 teaspoons baking powder
    1 teaspoon salt

Stir together and mix in sprouts.

    Oil for frying
    Lemon wedges

Drop batter by tablespoonfuls in hot oil. Deep-fry 3 to 5 minutes. Drain and serve hot with lemon wedges.

Serves 8

Sprout haters are plentiful, indeed, but this Southern dish is the best propaganda possible. Serve the fritters as a mystery dish, and after the second helpings are consumed, reveal the truth with a knowing smile.

BRAISED BRUSSELS SPROUTS

4 slices bacon

Fry until crisp. Remove, leaving grease in skillet. Crumble bacon.

½ cup diced onion
¼ cup sliced mushrooms

Sauté in bacon grease until onion is translucent.

3 cups small Brussels sprouts
Salt and pepper to taste

Add to skillet. Cover and cook 5 minutes. Turn off heat.

¼ cup grated cheddar cheese

Add. Stir to mix and melt. Serve sprinkled with bacon.

Serves 4

Yummy — much tastier with the small sprouts that come at the end of Brussels sprout season.

BRUSSELS SPROUTS
WITH ALMONDS

3 cups Brussels sprouts, cooked

Drain and keep warm.

3 tablespoons sour cream
2 tablespoons chopped almonds
2 tablespoons Parmesan cheese
1 tablespoon vermouth
¼ teaspoon nutmeg
¼ teaspoon dried tarragon
¼ teaspoon celery salt

Mix well and heat. Stir in sprouts.

Serves 4

BRUSSELS SPROUTS AND CELERY IN CHEESE SAUCE

   4   **cups Brussels sprouts**
1½ **cups chopped celery**
1½ **cups boiling water**
   1   **teaspoon salt**

Simmer in saucepan, 5 to 8 minutes. Drain and keep vegetables warm.

   4   **tablespoons butter**
   4   **tablespoons flour**

Melt butter, stir in flour, and cook, stirring, for several minutes.

1¾ **cups hot milk**
   1   **tablespoon grated onion**
  ½ **cup grated Swiss cheese**
      Dash of nutmeg

Add to roux and stir until thickened and cheese is melted. Stir warm sprouts into sauce.

Serves 6

BRUSSELS SPROUTS
WITH CHESTNUTS

2 dozen chestnuts

Make a cross on flat side of chestnuts. Roast 20 minutes at 350°. Shell and peel bitter inner skin. Simmer in water 45 minutes until soft.

4 cups cooked Brussels sprouts
5 tablespoons butter

Mix chestnuts and sprouts with butter. Heat and serve.

Serves 6

A traditional French holiday dish. Chestnuts are incredible trouble, but craved by a few experienced palates.

CABBAGE

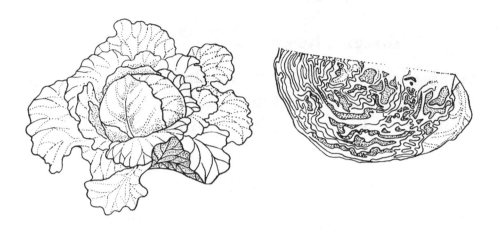

Cabbage frequently brings to mind dishes of a mundane peasant atmosphere. This is no coincidence: cabbage is the most ancient vegetable known today. Cultivated for more than 4,000 years, cabbage is the direct descendant of the wild cabbage (*brassica oleracea*) native to Western Europe. It was brought to Canada in the sixteenth century by an early colonist.

There are three kinds of cabbage: green smooth-leaved; red smooth-leaved; and green curly-leaved, or Savoy. Chinese or celery cabbage is not closely related to cabbage. Its leaves and stalk are more like lettuce, and it is usually eaten raw.

The Growing All members of the cabbage family are cool-season growers. Cabbage takes 40 to 110 days to mature. The gardener can choose from among early-maturing, midseason, or late cabbage in keeping with local climate. Early cabbage is cooked or used raw for coleslaw. The late varieties are preferred for sauerkraut. Remember that each plant bears only one large head, so thinning and spaced planting are essential. Few people want twenty heads of mature cabbage at once. Early-maturing varieties sometimes crack easily. Go ahead and harvest these, but try to use them quickly. If a nearly mature cabbage is threatened by hot or freezing weather, pull up the plant and store it in a cool dark place for a couple of weeks. Plant marigolds among cabbage plants; they are deterrents of the cabbage moth. To avoid recurring diseases, do not plant where cabbage relatives were planted the year before. Start early cabbage seeds indoors 4 to 6 weeks before transplanting to garden; set the plants 12 to 18 inches apart. Plant late cabbage seeds ¼ inch deep in ground at 6-inch intervals with rows spaced 3 feet apart. Thin to one plant every 2 feet.

The Harvest The cabbage head matures in the center of large, broad leaves. A head should be bright and glossy, firm and heavy for its size. It may weigh from 1 to 6 pounds, depending on the variety. Early cabbage tends to be smaller. The cabbage head is cut from the plant at the base of the head. Discard rest of plant after harvest.

The Basics

1–1½ pounds cabbage = ½ large head = 4 cups raw = 3 cups cooked = 4 servings.

1 cup shredded raw cabbage (3.5 ounces) = 24 calories, 5.4 grams carbohydrates, 1.3 grams protein, slightly more than the recommended daily vitamin C.

1 cup cooked cabbage (3.5 ounces) = 40 calories, 8 grams carbohydrates, 2 grams protein, slightly more than the recommended daily vitamin C.

1 cup shredded raw red cabbage (3.5 ounces) = 31 calories, 6.9 grams carbohydrates, 2 grams protein, twice the recommended daily vitamin C, some B.

1 cup shredded raw Savoy cabbage (3.5 ounces) = 24 calories 4.6 grams carbohydrates, 2.4 grams protein, almost twice the recommended daily vitamin C.

10-foot row = 5 plants.

Storage Soak cabbage in salted water if bugs are evident; otherwise refrigerate unwashed in plastic bag. Some varieties may be stored two months. (Commercial varieties will store only about two weeks.) Long storage causes loss of vitamins.

Freezing Cooked cabbage may be frozen, but it loses texture.

The Cooking Soak head in salty, cold water for 30 minutes to drive out insects, and increase crispness. Cut out stem and core within. Discard tough outer leaves. Cabbage may be cooked whole, in wedges, or shredded, and the cooking time varies accordingly. Red cabbage requires slightly longer cooking. It will become discolored when cooked unless vinegar or wine is added to the cooking water.

Basic Preparation Steam cabbage leaves 10 minutes or whole cabbage almost 1 hour. Serve with butter, salt, and freshly ground pepper. Shredded cabbage should be cooked with small amount of water several minutes. Serve with butter and lemon juice.

Complementary Herbs Allspice, celery seeds, cayenne pepper, and dill weed.

HEARTY CABBAGE BORSCHT

2¹/₂ **pounds stewing meat**
       dredged with flour

Brown in large heavy kettle.

1 **medium cabbage**

Cut into wedges, then thickly slice. Add to meat.

1 **cup tomato sauce**
1¹/₂ **cups water**
8 **large fresh tomatoes, peeled and**
    quartered, or a 1-pound
    13-ounce can
4 **carrots, sliced**
1 **large onion, diced**
   Juice of 3 lemons
2 **tablespoons salt**
²/₃ **cup sugar (or less)**
1 **clove garlic, minced**
1 **teaspoon dry mustard**
1 **tablespoon ketchup**
2 **potatoes, peeled and diced**
2 **cups cooked sliced beets**

Add to kettle, cover, and simmer 2 hours.

Serves 6

A meal in itself for a cold winter evening.

CABBAGE PATCH SOUP

1 medium head cabbage

Core and parboil about 8 minutes. Drain and separate leaves.

1½ pounds lean ground beef
1 onion, minced
1 egg, beaten
¼ cup soda cracker crumbs
½ clove garlic, minced
¼ teaspoon cinnamon
¼ teaspoon salt
½ cup uncooked rice

Mix well. Put 1 to 2 tablespoons in a cabbage leaf and roll up. Use largest leaves first, and continue until filling is used up. Arrange in a large kettle.

2½ cups V-3 juice (page 401) or
tomato juice
4 cups stewed tomatoes
1 cup tomato sauce

Mix together and pour over cabbage rolls. Cover and simmer 1½ hours.

Serves 6

Cabbage rolls pop up and down in a hearty tomato broth. Fun for kids or informal groups.

FAVORITE COLESLAW

1 **large head cabbage quartered, cored**
1 **green or red pepper**
1 **Bermuda onion**

Finely slice or dice into ½-inch cubes. Toss in a bowl to mix.

¾ **cup sugar**
1 **cup cider vinegar**
½ **cup salad oil**
1 **teaspoon celery seeds**
1 **teaspoon salt**
1 **teaspoon dry mustard**

Bring to a boil. Pour over salad ingredients. Chill.

Serves 6–8

BACON AND CABBAGE SALAD

4 slices bacon, chopped
1 small onion, finely chopped

Sauté.

1 teaspoon salt
1 teaspoon sugar
1 teaspoon celery seed
2 tablespoons vinegar
¼ cup mayonnaise

Add to bacon and onion.

1 small head cabbage, finely chopped
1 small green pepper, finely chopped

Pour dressing over. Mix lightly and serve at once.

Serves 6

PINEAPPLE-APPLE SLAW

- 3 **cups finely shredded cabbage**
- 1 **cup chopped apple**
- 1 **cup pineapple tidbits**
- ½ **cup chopped peanuts**
- ½ **cup finely chopped celery**
- 2 **bananas, sliced**

Combine in large bowl.

- ½ **cup mayonnaise and/or sour cream**
- 1 **tablespoon pineapple juice**
- 1 **tablespoon honey**
- 2 **squeezes lemon juice**
- ½ **cup raisins (optional)**

Mix in. Toss well.

Serves 6

This is a fun departure from ordinary coleslaw, and a great favorite with children.

SHREDDED CABBAGE WITH OLD-FASHIONED DRESSING

$^1/_3$ cup white vinegar
2 tablespoons olive oil
2 eggs beaten
2 tablespoons sugar
1 teaspoon mustard
$^1/_8$ teaspoon salt
Dash of pepper
Dash of Tabasco

Mix together in a saucepan and simmer, stirring until thick and creamy.

4 cups shredded cabbage
3 green onions, minced

Pour dressing over, toss, and chill.

Serves 4–6

CABBAGE ROLLS

1 medium head cabbage

Core and parboil in salted water 4 to 8 minutes, until outer leaves are soft. Drain. Peel off 12 large leaves.

2 small carrots
½ onion
1½ pounds ground beef, browned and drained
1 egg
¾ teaspoon salt
½ teaspoon thyme
¼ cup uncooked rice

Grate carrots and onions into pan with beef. Add rest of ingredients and stir well. Divide mixture into 12 parts. Stuff leaves and put smooth side up in shallow buttered casserole.

1 cup tomato sauce
¼ cup vinegar
½ cup brown sugar

Mix and pour over casserole.

2 tablespoons butter

Dot top of casserole with butter, cover with foil and bake at 375° for 35 minutes. Uncover and bake 20 minutes more.

Serves 6

STUFFED WHOLE CABBAGE

1 **large head cabbage**

Steam cabbage about 20 minutes until leaves are flexible. Do not overcook. Drain.

¾ **pound ground chuck**
¾ **pound ground pork**
2 **eggs**
2 **garlic cloves, minced**
1 **onion, chopped**
½ **cup rye cracker crumbs**
½ **teaspoon anchovy paste**
1½ **tablespoons ground coriander**
1½ **teaspoons dried thyme**
1 **teaspoon salt**
   Dash of ground cloves
   Dash of ground pepper

Mix well and form into small meatballs. To stuff cabbage, carefully separate leaves without breaking them off. Place a meatball in the center of the cabbage, then stuff a small meatball at the base of each leaf. Work in a circle from the center out; as each leaf is stuffed, lay it toward the center. Tie the cabbage with string to hold its shape.

4 **cups tomato purée**
¼ **teaspoon crushed dried hot peppers**
1½ **teaspoons dried thyme**
¾ **cup red wine**
2 **tablespoons minced scallions**

99

Mix in a Dutch oven. Place cabbage in sauce. Cover. Cook at 350° for 2 hours. Baste occasionally. To serve, cut in wedges.

Serves 6

Spectacular. The cabbage looks like a rose in bloom.

PASTEL DE COL

2 tablespoons olive oil
1 large yellow onion, chopped
1 green pepper, chopped

Sauté in large skillet.

1 pound ground round beef
¾ pound pork sausage

Add to skillet, brown, drain.

1 large head green cabbage

Core and steam 1 hour until medium soft, then separate the leaves. Line a 2-quart mold with largest leaves, overlapping them and extending above top of mold.

3 eggs, beaten
¼ teaspoon salt
Dash of pepper

Season eggs. Place a third of the meat mixture in mold, then a third of the eggs, then a layer of cabbage leaves. Repeat twice. Fold extended cabbage leaves over top. Cover mold and steam 1½ hours. Let cool about 10 minutes and unmold.

Serves 6

Unbeknownst to many, the Mexicans are quite fond of cabbage and make use of it frequently. This is just as delicious cold or reheated.

SWEET-SOUR RED CABBAGE

6 cups sliced red cabbage
3 tablespoons bacon grease
2 tablespoons chopped onion
6 tablespoons brown sugar
3 tablespoons vinegar

Sauté over slow heat for 18 minutes.

Serves 4–6

Serve this German dish with sauerbraten and potato pancakes.

CORNED BEEF AND CABBAGE SUMMER STYLE

3 medium potatoes

Cook 30 minutes, or until tender. Peel and cube while still warm.

2 tablespoons red wine vinegar
2 teaspoons celery seeds
2 teaspoons sugar
1/2 teaspoon salt

Drizzle vinegar and celery seeds over warm potatoes. Sprinkle with sugar and salt. Chill.

2 cups shredded cabbage
1/4 cup sliced green onion
1/2 cup chopped dill pickle
1 teaspoon prepared mustard
   Mayonnaise to taste
1/2 teaspoon salt
1 1/3 cups (12 ounce can) corned beef, cubed

Toss with potatoes.

Serves 6–8

Thoroughly delightful. Corned-beef-and-cabbage aficionados should relish this opportunity to enjoy a classic winter dish in such a refreshing manner all summer. This is one of those rare salads-in-a-meal that are really filling.

CABBAGE WEDGES
WITH MEAT SAUCE

1 **large head cabbage, cored and**
   cut into 6 wedges
¼ **teaspoon salt**

Place in a skillet, pour boiling water over, cover and cook 10 minutes until tender-crisp. Drain and keep warm.

½ **pound lean ground pork, chopped**
½ **onion, minced**
1 **green pepper, minced**
1 **clove garlic, minced**

Sauté, while stirring, until pork browns and begins to sizzle.

1 **cup tomato sauce**
1 **cup tomato paste**
½ **teaspoon salt**
1 **cup water**
½ **teaspoon dried oregano**

Add to skillet and simmer 15 to 20 minutes, stirring occasionally. Pour sauce over cabbage wedges.

Serves 4–6

CABBAGE STRUDEL

 1 **medium cabbage, shredded**
 1 **red onion, minced**
 ½ **cup butter**

Sauté 20 minutes in large skillet.

 ¾ **cup sugar**
 ½ **cup raisins**
    Juice and grated rind of
       ½ small lemon
 ½ **teaspoon cinnamon**
 ¼ **teaspoon nutmeg**

Add to skillet and simmer 15 to 20 minutes until liquid is absorbed. Remove from heat.

 6 **leaves phyllo pastry**
 ½ **cup butter, melted**
 ½ **cup graham cracker crumbs**

Layer leaves of phyllo with butter and crumbs. Spread filling on left side of dough and roll lengthwise like a jelly roll. Bake on buttered sheet 20 to 30 minutes at 350°.

Serves 8

Ready-made sheets of strudel or phyllo pastry are now available in most metropolitan areas.

CARROTS

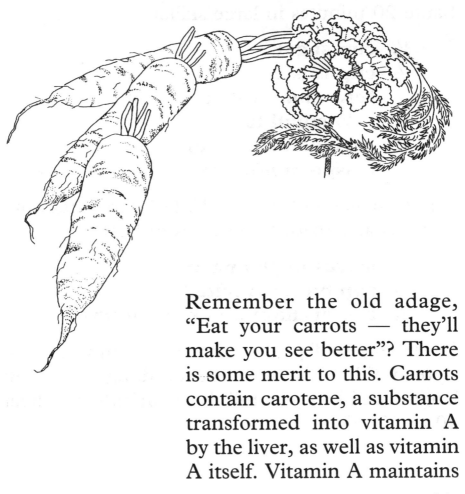

Remember the old adage, "Eat your carrots — they'll make you see better"? There is some merit to this. Carrots contain carotene, a substance transformed into vitamin A by the liver, as well as vitamin A itself. Vitamin A maintains healthy eyesight, pervents night blindness, and is important in bone and teeth formation.

Carrots have always been an important crop. They are reliable to grow, can tolerate chilly weather, store well without refrigeration, and supply the minimum daily recommended supply of vitamin A. But they have not always been the familiar orange color. The Europeans grew purple carrots.

The Growing The carrot is really a biennial, although treated as an annual. If the carrot is left in the ground, the second year it will produce pretty foliage, with white blossoms much like its ancestor, the wild flower Queen Anne's lace. Carrots may be planted around the periphery of the garden for show. They take 65 to 75 days to mature, and remember to plan for successive crops. Carrots are hardy, but they are fussy about their garden home. They need loose soil in order to grow fast and deep. They will stay short and stumpy in heavy soil. Mix in loam and peat deeply for long straight carrots. If the soil is inhibitive, select some of the shorter varieties. Carrots prefer cool weather, tolerating temperatures as low as 25 degrees. Carrot seeds are slow to germinate (taking about 2 weeks), but must be planted directly in the ground. Sprinkle seeds in rows spaced 1 foot apart at a depth of ½ inch. Young seedlings are very tiny and difficult to see. When carrots get crowded, thin to 2 inches apart.

The Harvest Carrots are frequently the favorite harvest of children. They are one of the few crops that they can harvest and eat on the spot. An average carrot is about 7 inches in length, and the shorter varieties are 4 to 5 inches (and fatter).

Carrots are ready to pull when the orange top pops its head above the ground. Pull them out at the base of their foliage. Children enjoy putting the bare carrot tops in a dish of water; new foliage shoots up as the small plants root.

The Basics
1 pound = 8 six-inch carrots = 2 cups sliced = 4 servings.
1 large raw carrot (3.5 ounces) = 42 calories, 9.7 grams carbohydrates, 1.1 grams protein, almost 3 times recommended daily vitamin A.
$^2/_3$ cup cooked (3.5 ounces) = 31 calories, 7.1 grams carbohydrates, .9 gram protein, $2^1/_2$ times recommended daily vitamin A.
One 10-foot row = about 75 carrots.

The Storage Carrots store better in the ground than in the refrigerator. Leave them until ready for use. To refrigerate, remove greens, rinse, and store in plastic bags up to 2 weeks.

Freezing If whole, scald 5 minutes; if cut, scald $3^1/_2$ minutes. Plunge in ice water to stop cooking. Drain, package, label, and freeze.

The Cooking Scrub young carrots with a brush. Peel older carrots with a vegetable peeler. Remember that garden-fresh carrots cook faster than store-bought ones.

Basic Preparation Boil whole large carrots 20

minutes, small or cut carrots 8 to 10 minutes. Sauté shredded carrots 4 to 6 minutes. Sliced carrots can be wrapped in foil, dotted with butter, and baked in the oven for 30 minutes.

Complementary Herbs Basil, chives, ginger, mint and parsley.

CHILLED CARROT VICHYSSOISE

   3 **medium potatoes, peeled and diced**
   4 **large carrots, diced**
  ½ **cup strong chicken stock**

Simmer covered until vegetables are tender, 10 to 15 minutes. Remove 1 cup vegetables; mince them. Pour rest of ingredients into the blender.

   1 **cup cream**
   1 **teaspoon salt**
      Squeeze of lemon juice

Add to blender and purée. Stir in minced vegetables. Chill.

Serves 4

Serve in icy-clear glass bowls to allow the pale orange color to shine. Garnish with minced chives or mint.

CARROT SOUP

3 cups chicken stock
1 small onion, chopped
4 carrots, peeled and sliced
$^1/_8$ teaspoon nutmeg
2 tablespoons peanut butter
1 tablespoon Worcestershire sauce
1 clove garlic, minced
Dash of Tabasco

Simmer until tender, about 15 minutes. Remove half of carrots. Purée rest of ingredients. Add reserved carrots, and reheat before serving.

Serves 4

Definitely unique, this has an Indian flavor. Garnish with chopped peanuts, apples, and green onions.

MARINATED CARROT SALAD

6–8 large carrots, sliced on diagonal

Parboil 3 to 5 minutes and drain.

½ cup olive oil
¼ cup white wine vinegar
½ red onion, sliced
2 cloves garlic, minced
1 teaspoon fresh chopped basil
1 teaspoon salt
½ teaspoon pepper
Juice of 1 lemon

Mix all and pour over carrots. Refrigerate overnight.

1 large head butter or Boston lettuce

Arrange on lettuce leaves to serve.

Serves 6

Also great as an hors d'oeuvre. Cut small new carrots on slant into generous 1-inch slices. Chill and serve with toothpicks.

CARROT SLAW

8–10 carrots
  1 green or red pepper
  1 Bermuda onion
  1 green apple (optional)
  1 cup raisins (optional)

Shred all except raisins. Mix together.

$1/_3$ cup sugar
$1/_2$ cup cider vinegar
$1/_4$ cup salad oil
$1/_2$ teaspoon celery seeds
$1/_2$ teaspoon dry mustard
$1/_2$ teaspoon salt

Combine and bring to a boil. Pour over salad. Chill.

Serves 6–8

GLAZED CARROTS

6 young carrots, cut in 2-inch fingers

Cook barely covered in water 15 to 20 minutes. Drain, reserving ½ cup liquid.

4 tablespoons butter
2 tablespoons brown sugar
¾ teaspoon salt

Add to cooked carrots in saucepan along with reserved carrot liquid. Stir gently over low heat to glaze carrots.

Serves 4

Secret: Serve this to carrot-hating children and call it carrot candy.

CARROTS IN MINT SAUCE

6 carrots, diced, sliced, or slivered

Parboil, covered, in small quantity of boiling water 5 to 8 minutes. Drain, reserving $1/3$ cup liquid.

2 tablespoons butter

Melt in saucepan.

1 tablespoon sugar
1 teaspoon cornstarch
$1/8$ teaspoon salt

Mix and stir into butter.

Juice and grated rind of $1/2$ lemon
1 tablespoon shredded fresh
mint leaves

Add along with reserved carrot liquid, and stir over heat just until thickened. Put carrots back into pan, heat, and toss gently to glaze.

Serves 4

Elegant as the English serve it, with roast lamb or chicken.

CARROT AND ZUCCHINI CASSEROLE

6 carrots
6 small zucchini

Slice into thin rounds. (Refrigerate if you want to prepare dish later.)

3 tablespoons butter
1 clove garlic, peeled
1 yellow onion, chopped
1 teaspoon salt
$^1/_8$ teaspoon pepper
$^3/_4$ teaspoon dried thyme
$^1/_4$ cup water

Sauté garlic in large skillet until brown, then discard garlic. Add onion and sauté 5 minutes. Season, add water, carrots and zucchini, stir, cover, and simmer gently 10 to 15 minutes.

$^1/_4$–$^1/_2$ cup grated Parmesan cheese
Chopped fresh parsley

Sprinkle with cheese. Garnish with parsley.

Serves 6

CARROTS AU MADÈRE

10 carrots, cut into ½-inch slices
10 small boiling onions, peeled
 5 ounces bacon, diced
 4 tablespoons butter

Sauté in Dutch oven until onions are golden.

1 bay leaf
   Pinch of dried thyme
   Salt and pepper to taste
6 tablespoons Madeira wine

Add, cover, and simmer over very low heat 25 to 30 minutes.

Minced fresh parsley

Place in serving bowl and sprinkle with parsley.

Serves 6

GINGERED CARROT CASSEROLE

12   medium carrots cut in ½-inch slices
¼   cup butter

Sauté for a few minutes.

½   cup light cream
 2   tablespoons brown sugar
¼   teaspoon powdered ginger
¼   teaspoon salt
¼   cup slivered almonds

Mix, then stir into carrots. Place in buttered casserole, cover, and bake at 350° for 30 minutes.

Serves 6

SPRING CARROT CASSEROLE

10–12 **medium carrots**
  1 **cup water**
  ½ **teaspoon salt**
  12 **whole scallions**

Cook carrots in covered saucepan with water for 9 minutes. Add salt and scallions and cook 3 more minutes. Drain. Slice carrots lengthwise. Place in buttered casserole.

  4 **tablespoons melted butter**
  ½ **teaspoon salt**
  2 **tablespoons honey**
    Dash of pepper
    Grated rind of ½ lemon
    Juice of ½ lemon

Mix, then simmer a few minutes. Pour over carrots. Heat covered in 350° oven for 15 minutes.

Serves 4–6

Light and pleasant. Complete this spring menu with leg of roasted lamb, fancy oven-baked potatoes, and a Bibb salad.

MOCK CARROT SOUFFLÉ

4 large carrots, cooked
1 cup carrot cooking liquid

Purée in blender.

12 soda crackers, mashed
1 tablespoon butter, melted
2 teaspoons grated onion
¾ cup grated mild cheese

Mix with carrots.

Grated Parmesan cheese

Dust buttered soufflé dish with Parmesan, add carrot mixture, and bake at 350° for 20 minutes.

Serves 4

Great for very young children!

CARROT COOKIES

1 cup softened butter or margarine
¾ cup sugar

Cream together.

1 egg, beaten
1½ cups shredded raw carrots
½ teaspoon vanilla

Add to mixture.

2 cups flour
2 teaspoons baking powder
½ teaspoon salt

Sift into mixture and blend. Drop by teaspoonfuls onto greased cookie sheets. Bake about 10 minutes at 375°.

1 cup confectioner's sugar
  Grated rind of 1 orange
  Juice of 1 orange (just enough to moisten)

Cream together and frost cookies.

3 dozen

A tea cookie. So-o-o good!

RAISIN-CARROT COOKIES

½ **cup boiling water**
½ **cup raisins**

Combine, let stand 5 minutes, then drain.

1 **cup brown sugar**
½ **cup softened butter**
1 **egg**
1 **teaspoon lemon extract**
1 **cup finely shredded raw carrots**

Mix with raisins.

1½ **cups flour**
2 **teaspoons baking powder**
½ **teaspoon salt**

Sift into mixture. Stir just until moist. Drop by teaspoonfuls onto greased cookie sheet. Bake at 400° for 10 to 12 minutes.

3 dozen

Fill your cookie jar with these after-school snacks.

CARROT SPONGE CAKE

   3 **cups shredded carrots**
   4 **egg yolks**
   2 **cups sugar**
1½ **cups oil**

Combine in large bowl.

   2 **cups flour**
   3 **teaspoons cinnamon**
   2 **teaspoons soda**
 ½ **teaspoon salt**

Sift together three times, then add to carrot mixture.

   4 **egg whites, stiffly beaten**

Fold into batter. Pour into three 10-inch pans or four 8-inch pans. Bake at 350° for 20 to 30 minutes. Frost as desired.

Serves 6

CARROT CAKE

    2   cups flour
    1   teaspoon salt
    1   teaspoon nutmeg
    1   teaspoon cinnamon
 1½   teaspoons baking soda
    2   teaspoons baking powder

Sift together into large bowl.

 1½   cups oil
    2   cups sugar
    4   eggs, slightly beaten

Mix together and add to dry ingredients.

    2   cups grated raw carrots
    1   cup drained crushed pineapple
    1   cup chopped nuts

Add to batter. Pour into greased Bundt pan and bake 1 hour at 325°. Or use greased 13-by-9-inch pan for 30 to 35 minutes.

    8   ounces cream cheese,
            at room temperature
    1   box confectioner's sugar
    1   teaspoon vanilla extract
  12   tablespoons butter or margarine,
            at room temperature

Cream together, and frost cake when cool.

Serves 8

To decorate, wash and dry a carrot with greens still attached and lay on top of cake.

CARROT TEA CAKE

  1 **cup sugar**
$^2/_3$ **cup softened butter**

Cream together.

  1 **cup grated raw carrots**
  2 **eggs, beaten**
$^1/_2$ **cup chopped pecans**

Stir in.

1$^1/_2$ **cups flour**
  1 **teaspoon baking powder**
  1 **teaspoon baking soda**
  1 **teaspoon cinnamon**
$^1/_4$ **teaspoon salt**

Sift in and mix until blended. Bake at 325° for 1 hour in a greased 1$^1/_2$-quart loaf pan.

Makes 1 loaf

CARROT MARMALADE

4 medium lemons
2 medium oranges

Grate peels, then remove white part and thinly slice fruit.

4 carrots, shredded
6 cups sugar

Add to peel and fruit and bring to a hard boil. Boil 2 minutes.

3 ounces fruit pectin

Boil 2 more minutes, stirring in pectin. Stir while cooking. Ladle into sterilized glasses and cover with paraffin.

3 pints

A longtime favorite at state fairs and a delightful Christmas gift. This is perfect on homemade biscuits for Sunday breakfast.

CAULIFLOWER

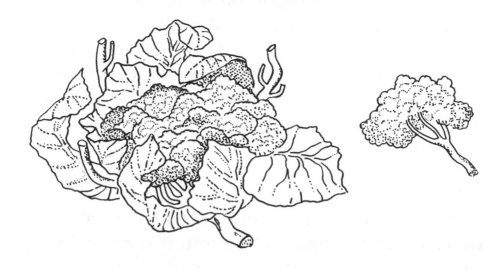

The word "cauliflower" is derived from the Latin, *caulis floris,* meaning cabbage flower. The edible portion of the cauliflower plant is a tight head, usually white, of flower buds. Cauliflower is another member of the cabbage family. Although the cabbage family is very old, there is no record of cauliflower until the twelfth century. A Moslem-Spanish gardener described it and referred to it as Syrian cabbage.

The Growing Cauliflower is the most temperamental of the cole crops and will not head if the temperature goes above 75°. It cannot withstand frost. The white-head varieties require 3 to 3½ months from sowing to harvest, which really prohibits cauliflower production in many areas. Plants started indoors take 60 to 80 days to mature. For the cool, humid climate the purple-

127

headed variety is a fun experiment. It turns green when cooked and tastes more like broccoli. Beware, however, as it takes slightly more than 4 months to grow from seed. Seeds are slow to germinate and grow. Start seeds indoors in peat pots. They require a month to reach transplanting size. Transplant in rows spaced 3 feet apart, setting plants at 2-foot intervals.

The Harvest The cauliflower plant grows about 2½ feet tall. Because of the wide spacing required, and its slow maturation, it is a good idea to plant fast-growing crops in between, such as lettuce or carrots. Or plant onions or dill nearby, as they are good repellents of insects.

The bud head, or curd, grows from the center on a stalk. To ensure whiteness of the curd, the surrounding jacket leaves should be tied around it with string when it is about 3 inches across (purple cauliflower does not need this blanching). It will be ready to harvest 2 to 3 weeks later. Cut the head where it meets the main stem. Pull out and discard the plant. If weather threatens to bolt or freeze cauliflower, pull up the plant and hang it upside down in a cool dark place for a couple of weeks. A bolting cauliflower acquires a yellowish tint and has spreading florets.

The Basics
1 pound = 1 4-inch head = 4 cups florets = 5 servings.
1 cup raw chopped cauliflower (3.5 ounces) = 27

calories, 5.2 grams carbohydrates, 2.7 grams protein, 2 times recommended daily vitamin C.

$7/_8$ cup cooked chopped cauliflower (3.5 ounces) = 22 calories, 4.1 grams carbohydrates, 2.3 grams protein, almost 2 times recommended daily vitamin C.

50-foot row = 25 plants = 25 heads.

The Storage It is not necessary to wash before refrigeration. The head should be stored in a plastic bag and will keep 4 to 5 days without loss of freshness. Handle carefully, as cauliflower bruises easily.

Freezing Cut cauliflower into 1-inch segments. Soak 30 minutes in salted water. Scald 4 minutes. Chill in cold water, drain, package in bags of convenient size, label and freeze. (Cook frozen cauliflower in small amount of boiling water 4 minutes.)

The Cooking Remove jacket leaves and cut off stalks. Soak 30 minutes in salted water to drive out insects and ensure crispness. Cook it whole, or divide into florets. The jacket leaves and cut-up stalks of very fresh cauliflower may be cooked as well. A piece of lemon may be added to the cooking water to retain the whiteness.

Basic Preparation Steam whole cauliflower 20 to 30 minutes, florets 10 minutes, and serve with lemon butter, hollandaise, or cheese sauce. Small cauliflower florets may be sautéed in butter (with garlic) for 10 minutes.

Complementary Herbs Basil, caraway, coriander, garlic, thyme, turmeric.

CAULIFLOWER APPETIZERS

Serve cauliflower raw or steamed until tender-crisp, then chilled. Offer it as an appetizer with your favorite dip or one of the following:

Curried Mayonnaise

1   **cup mayonnaise**
    Juice of 1 lemon
¼   **teaspoon prepared mustard**
¼   **teaspoon curry powder**
    Capers, if desired

Mix together. Chill a few hours to blend flavors.

Guacamole

1   **avocado, mashed**
    Juice of ½ lemon
½   **tomato, juiced, seeded, and**
        finely chopped
3   **green onions, minced**
    Pinch of crushed dried red peppers
    Dash of Tabasco

Blend well together. Serve immediately or cover tightly to prevent surface from darkening.

Chive Hollandaise

  1 **cup hollandaise sauce (p. 455)**
½ **cup sour cream**
    Juice of ¼ lemon
  1 **tablespoon minced chives**

Heat gently, stirring until smooth. Serve hot or chilled.

CREAM OF CAULIFLOWER SOUP

1 large head cauliflower
1 chicken bouillon cube
½ lemon, cut into 2 pieces

Cut cauliflower into florets and put in large kettle. Add water to cover. Cook until tender, 10 to 15 minutes. Drain. Set aside 1½ cups cauliflower and discard lemon. Pour rest of cauliflower into blender and purée.

3 tablespoons butter
3 tablespoons flour

Melt butter, stir in flour, and cook, stirring for several minutes. Add purée and stir.

1½ cups milk
½ teaspoon salt (or more to taste)
¼ teaspoon nutmeg (or more to taste)

Add to purée. Heat and stir until thickened. Chop and add the reserved florets to soup.

Serves 6

Rich and yummy.

CAULIFLOWER SALAD
WITH CHIVE CREAM

1   **large cauliflower, cut into florets**
½   **lemon**

Steam together 15 to 20 minutes, until tender-crisp. Drain. Discard lemon.

½   **cup minced fresh parsley**
1   **tablespoon minced chives**
½   **cup sour cream**
2   **tablespoons wine vinegar**
3   **tablespoons olive oil**
1   **tablespoon lemon juice**
1   **teaspoon prepared mustard**

Mix together. Toss with cauliflower. Chill and serve.

Serves 4

CAULIFLOWER GARDEN SALAD

1   clove garlic, mashed
1   teaspoon salt
2   tablespoons lemon juice
$^1/_4$ teaspoon sugar
$^1/_4$ teaspoon pepper
$^1/_8$ teaspoon celery seeds
$^1/_4$–$^1/_2$ teaspoon paprika
$^3/_4$ teaspoon dry mustard
5   tablespoons olive oil

Mix all and chill.

$^1/_2$ head cauliflower, cut into florets
1   head of lettuce, crisped and torn
1   bunch watercress, torn
1   tomato, peeled and sliced
$^1/_2$ avocado, diced
$^1/_2$ cup slivered toasted almonds

Combine in bowl and toss with dressing.

Serves 6

MOM'S STANDBY CAULIFLOWER

  1 **cauliflower**
  ½ **lemon**

Cover with boiling water and steam 20 to 30 minutes until tender-crisp. Drain. Discard lemon.

  ¼ **cup butter, cut in slices**
  1 **cup crushed crackers**
  ½ **cup grated Parmesan cheese**
  ½ **cup toasted slivered almonds**
      (optional)

Stick butter slices into cauliflower. Sprinkle with rest of ingredients. Bake until warm in 350° oven.

Serves 4

CAULIFLOWER ANTIPASTO

  1 **medium head cauliflower**
3–4 **carrots**

Cut cauliflower into bite-size florets and slice carrots $1/2$ inch thick. Place in a large kettle.

  $2/3$ **cup vinegar**
  $2/3$ **cup water**
  $1/4$ **cup vegetable oil**
  1 **tablespoon olive oil**
$1^1/_2$ **tablespoons sugar**
  1 **clove garlic, mashed**
  1 **teaspoon dried oregano**
      Generous dashes of salt and
          freshly ground pepper

Add to kettle, cover, and bring to a boil. Simmer 8 to 10 minutes. Cool and refrigerate 1 to 2 days.

Serves 6

Very easy and nice to have for low-calorie nibbling or to serve for a cocktail party. Make a day or so ahead so flavors have time to blend.

CAULIFLOWER AMANDINE

1   cauliflower, cut into florets
½   lemon

Cook, covered, in boiling water until tender (20 to 30 minutes). Drain. Discard lemon.

1   cup milk
2   tablespoons butter
2   tablespoons flour
½   cup grated cheddar cheese
¼   cup minced green onions (optional)
Toasted almonds

Melt butter, stir in flour, and cook, stirring for several minutes. Pour in milk, stir until smooth, then add cheese and onions. Cook gently, stirring, until cheese melts. Pour over cauliflower and sprinkle with almonds.

Serves 4

This is basically cauliflower with cheese sauce. The almonds and green onions add an extra zing to a traditional approach.

HOT BRAISED CAULIFLOWER

4–6 tablespoons vegetable oil
1–1½ teaspoons finely chopped
fresh ginger
¾ teaspoon turmeric
¼ teaspoon cayenne pepper
1½ teaspoons ground coriander
1 clove garlic, minced

Mix to paste. Heat in large skillet.

1 head of cauliflower, broken up
½ cup water

Add to skillet. Cover and cook about 10 minutes.
Stir occasionally. Add more water if necessary.

Serves 4

*Frozen cauliflower will not work with this recipe —
it must be fresh and crisp to sauté. The cauliflower
becomes a warm umber color because of the turmeric.
It is a spicy dish which would go nicely with roasted
leg of lamb and buttered, steamed chard or spinach.
Use any cold leftover cauliflower in a green salad.*

FROSTED CAULIFLOWER

1 large head of cauliflower

Steam 20 to 25 minutes until tender-crisp. Drain.

½ cup mayonnaise
1½ teaspoons prepared mustard
2 teaspoons grated onion
1 cup shredded cheddar cheese
Dash of salt

Mix together and frost cauliflower. Bake at 350° for 10 to 15 minutes to melt cheese.

Serves 4

WHIPPED CAULIFLOWER

1 medium cauliflower, cut into florets

Cook until tender, 20 to 30 minutes. Drain.

$^1/_3$ **cup milk**
1 egg, beaten
**4 tablespoons grated mild cheese
     (Bonbel, Swiss, Gouda)
    Salt and pepper to taste**
2 tablespoons butter

Place with cauliflower in mixing bowl, and beat to purée.

**Fresh bread crumbs
Butter**

Put mixture in greased loaf pan. Sprinkle with bread crumbs and dot with butter. Bake at 350° for 20 minutes.

Serves 4

Very rich tasting. It is like mashed potatoes, although more intriguing.

CAULIFLOWER LOAF

4 **cups grated cauliflower**
½ **cup grated almonds**
½ **cup rich chicken stock**
½ **cup fresh bread crumbs**
    (whole wheat preferably)
1 **cup grated cheddar cheese**
1 **egg**
    Salt and pepper to taste

Combine in a blender or mix well by hand. Bake for 30 minutes in a greased loaf pan at 350°.

Serves 8

This has an unusual taste, quite different from plain cauliflower. It tastes somewhat like stuffing and is compatible with poultry. It can be frozen.

CAULIFLOWER FRITTERS

1 medium cauliflower

Break into florets. Slice large florets in half.

2 eggs, beaten
½ cup flour
½ cup light cream
½ teaspoon salt
Dash of pepper
2 tablespoons melted butter

Mix well with whisk or blender.

Oil for deep frying
Grated Parmesan cheese

Dip florets into batter. Fry in hot oil, 4 or 5 at a time. Drain on paper towels. Sprinkle with cheese.

Serves 8

Serve immediately or refrigerate and reheat on baking sheet in 350° oven for about 10 minutes until hot. Cauliflower fritters make an interesting hot hors d'oeuvre. Frozen cauliflower will be too soggy for this.

CAULIFLOWER WITH HAM

2 **tablespoons oil**
1 **clove garlic**
2 **teaspoons minced fresh ginger**

Sauté in large skillet. Discard garlic.

1 **cauliflower cut into florets, then halved**
6 **green onions sliced diagonally**
1½ **cups slivered cooked ham**

Add to skillet. Stir about 5 minutes over high heat.

¾ **cup chicken stock**
1 **tablespoon cornstarch**
   Dash of salt
2 **teaspoons soy sauce**

Mix together and pour into skillet. Stir constantly over medium heat until thickened.

Serves 4

Serve this Chinese dish with brown rice, mandarin orange avocado salad, and chopsticks!

CHARD

Chard is the oldest member of the beet family and is grown for its tasty leaves and stalks; the root is inedible. Red chard has changed little over the last 2,000 years. The green and yellow varieties of chard developed later and were described by a Swiss botanist in the sixteenth century. It has since been popularly known as Swiss chard.

Chard consists of a large rib section which grows up into the leafy green. The rib section tastes something like a cross between celery and asparagus. The leafy part is much like spinach. Usually, the rib area is cut out and cooked 5 minutes more than the leaf. Sometimes the ribs are served separately. Chard can be green-leafed with a white stem or have red stalks resembling rhubarb. The leaves are always crinkly.

The Growing Chard will flourish when all else in the garden fails until the winter gets too severe. It will grow in weather too hot for spinach or lettuce, and it can tolerate temperatures as low as 35°. It requires 60 days from sowing to full maturation, but the leaves may be harvested well before that. Pick off any flowers that may appear: they go to seed, and the plant stops producing leaves. Sow the seeds 1 inch deep in rows spaced 1½ feet apart. When seedlings reach about 2 inches, thin to 4 inches apart. Thin again when plants are 7 inches tall to space plants about 8 inches apart. It is best to thin twice to maximize the thinnings yield. The thinnings are delicious steamed and tossed with butter.

The Harvest Chard leaves may be harvested all summer. Cut off outer leaves near base; leave the new inner leaves; never strip the plant. Harvest leaves frequently to keep plant producing. If the outer leaves are not removed, chard will stop growing.

The Basics
1 pound = 1 large bunch = 16 medium leaves = 4 cups raw = 1 cup cooked.
1 cup cooked (3.5 ounces) = 35 calories, 6 grams carbohydrates, 3.5 grams protein, twice the recommended daily vitamin A, the daily vitamin C, and many minerals.
10-foot row = 10 plants.

The Storage Wash leaves. Shake off most of the moisture. Store in the refrigerator in a plastic bag with a few pieces of paper toweling for 3 to 5 days.

Freezing Wash well. Scald ribs 1 minute. Add leaves and scald for 3 more minutes. Chill in ice water. Drain. Chop, if desired. Package with water that clings. Label and freeze.

The Cooking Chard may be boiled or sautéed quickly. It is not suitable for raw salads. The cooking softens the strong leafy taste that is objectionable in the raw state.

Basic Preparation Wash thoroughly. Cut out rib sections. Cook ribs in boiling salted water 5 minutes. Then add leafy part and boil another 7 minutes. Chop if desired. (The chopping may be done before the cooking, if preferred.) May be served with butter and lemon juice, or hollandaise.

Complementary Herbs Basil, garlic, nutmeg, oregano.

CHARD VICHYSSOISE

 2 **tablespoons butter**
 1 **large onion, minced**
 3 **medium potatoes, peeled and diced**
12–14 **leaves chard, washed and diced**

Sauté 15 minutes in large skillet.

 2 **tablespoons flour**

Stir into skillet.

 3 **cups chicken stock**
 2 **cups shredded cheddar cheese**
 ½ **teaspoon salt**
    Juice of ½ lemon

Stir in, bring to boil, reduce heat.

 1 **cup milk**
    Dash of nutmeg or thyme (optional)

Stir in. Check seasoning. Serve hot or cold.

Serves 6

GARLIC CREAMED CHARD

4 cups chopped and cooked chard

1 large onion, chopped
2 cloves garlic, minced
2 tablespoons butter

Sauté until soft. Add chard. Sauté 1 minute.

½ cup heavy cream
¼ teaspoon ground nutmeg

Stir in over low heat. Heat well, but do not boil.

½ cup grated Parmesan cheese
  Salt and freshly ground pepper

Add half of cheese. Season to taste. Place in serving bowl and sprinkle rest of cheese on top.

Serves 6

This dish may be prepared ahead, placed in a casserole, covered, and chilled. Then bake uncovered in a 375° oven for 20 to 30 minutes.

CHARD AND TOMATOES

2 tablespoons olive oil
1 onion, diced
2 cloves garlic, minced

Sauté until golden in large skillet.

3 large tomatoes, peeled and diced
½ cup chopped cooked ham (optional)
2 cups cooked chopped chard

Stir in and heat until bubbly.

Butter
Salt and pepper
Nutmeg

Season to taste.

½ cup grated Parmesan cheese

Serve, sprinkling with cheese.

Serves 4

Easy and pretty.

JOE'S SPECIAL

    3 tablespoons olive oil
    1 pound lean ground beef
    1 large onion, minced
    ½ pound mushrooms, sliced

Sauté until beef is browned.

    4 cups chopped chard
    ½ teaspoon salt
       Dash of pepper

Add and stir lightly to cook chard.

    2 eggs, well beaten

Stir in, cooking until set.

Serves 4

A hearty red wine and crusty French bread complete this one-dish meal.

CHARD STIR-FRY

1 **clove garlic, peeled**
½ **onion, minced**
2 **tablespoons oil**

Sauté, then discard garlic.

6 **cups cut-up chard**

Add chard and stir-fry 3 minutes.

2 **tablespoons soy sauce**
½ **teaspoon sugar**
1 **6-ounce can water chestnuts,
   drained and sliced**

Add and simmer 3 minutes.

Serves 4

CHARD AND EGG CASSEROLE

4 **cups chopped cooked chard**
Butter
Salt and pepper

Cover bottom of shallow baking dish with chard. Dot with butter. Season to taste.

8 **eggs**
1 **cup Swiss cheese, grated**
Butter
Salt and pepper

Underfry eggs. Gently transfer to top of chard. Cover with cheese. Dot with butter. Sprinkle with seasonings. Broil until cheese melts.

Serves 4

A perfect choice for a meatless dinner. Chard, eggs, and cheese have a marvelous affinity for one another.

RICE VERDE

1 **cup cooked chopped chard**
2 **eggs, beaten**
1 **cup milk**
4 **tablespoons melted butter**
2 **teaspoons grated onion**
1 **teaspoon Worcestershire sauce**
$1^1/_2$ **teaspoons salt**
$^1/_3$ **cup fresh minced parsley**
$^1/_2$ **cup grated cheddar cheese**
3 **cups cooked rice**

Mix together and pour into buttered 2-quart casserole. Bake 45 minutes at 325°.

Serves 6

CHARD ON BAKED
SLICED TOMATOES

2 cups cooked chopped chard
$^1/_3$ minced green onion
4 tablespoons melted butter
$^1/_4$ teaspoon salt
$^1/_3$ cup grated Parmesan cheese
1 garlic clove, mashed
$^1/_2$ teaspoon dried thyme
2 eggs, beaten

Mix thoroughly.

3 large tomatoes
Salt and freshly ground pepper

Slice very thick and make single layer in greased baking dish. Season to taste.

$^1/_4$ **cup fresh bread crumbs**

Top tomatoes with mounds of chard and sprinkle with bread crumbs. Bake 15 minutes at 350°.

Serves 6–8

CHARD-STUFFED
MANICOTTI

10 manicotti shells

Cook in boiling, salted water 8 minutes. Drain.

10–12 chard leaves, finely chopped
¹/₄ pound mushrooms, diced
1 medium onion, finely chopped
3 tablespoons butter

Sauté over high heat. Remove from stove.

1 egg, beaten
1 cup ricotta cheese
¹/₄ cup grated Parmesan cheese
**2 six-ounce cans tuna, drained and
    flaked**
Juice of ¹/₂ lemon
¹/₄ teaspoon salt

Stir into chard mixture. Stuff into cooked shells.
Place in shallow casserole with any leftover filling
along sides.

3 tablespoons butter
3 tablespoons flour
1 cup chicken broth
1 cup milk

Melt butter, add flour and gradually stir in the
broth and milk. Stir and cook 5 minutes until
thickened.

$^1/_3$ **cup white wine**
   Grated Parmesan cheese

Add wine to sauce and pour over stuffed shells. Sprinkle with Parmesan. Bake at 350° for 30 minutes.

Serves 6

A meatless main dish, inexpensive and tasty.

CHARD-SAUSAGE STUFFING

3 cups cooked brown or wild rice
3 cups cooked chopped chard
1 pound ground sausage, cooked
 (reserve drippings)

Combine in large bowl.

Drippings from sausage
½ cup chopped celery
½ cup chopped onion
1 clove garlic, minced
2 tablespoons minced fresh parsley
½ teaspoon dried rosemary
½ teaspoon dried basil
½ teaspoon dried sage
½ teaspoon salt

Sauté, and then simmer 10 minutes.

4 tablespoons butter

Add to skillet and stir until melted. Pour all over rice mixture. Moisten with water if too dry.

Stuffs a 12-pound turkey or 4 roasting chickens

Reputed to have brought fame to an old-time San Francisco restaurant.

CHARD-POTATO BAKE

**3 cups sliced cooked potatoes
(Idaho or new potatoes best)
5 carrots, cooked and sliced
3 cups cooked chopped chard mixed
with ½ cup grated Swiss cheese**

Butter baking dish. Layer half of potatoes, carrots, chard and cheese. Repeat.

**4 tablespoons butter, cut up
Fresh bread crumbs
1 tablespoon grated Swiss cheese**

Sprinkle over casserole. Bake at 350° for 20 minutes.

Serves 6

A great family dish. Double or triple the recipe for large groups.

CORN

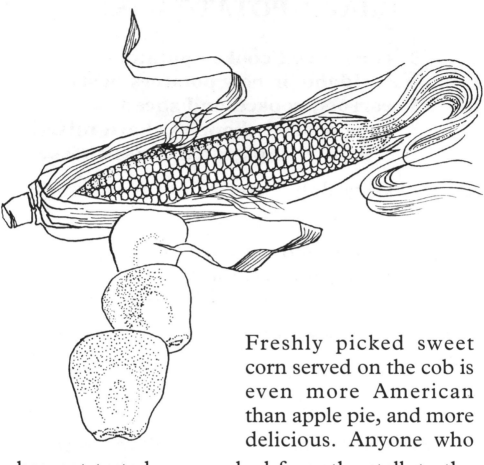

Freshly picked sweet corn served on the cob is even more American than apple pie, and more delicious. Anyone who has not tasted corn rushed from the stalk to the boiling pot may not understand what the fuss is all about. Corn loses sugar faster than any other vegetable. Even after the passage of an hour, particularly on a hot day, a great deal of sweetness is lost. The ecstasy of fresh sweet corn was truly appreciated by the American Indians, who thought that corn came from the gods. The Mayans erected a corn god in the corn fields, as do some Indian farmers in Mexico today.

There are hundreds of varieties and hybrids of corn. The hybrids are more productive and disease-resistant; however, there are some tradition lovers who claim nothing is as sweet as the old-fashioned Golden Bantam. Corn can be yellow, white, yellow/white, white/black, red, or black. The black varieties are very hard to find. Yellow is considered to be the sweetest and most nutritious.

The Growing Corn is an annual which requires a lot of space and sun. At least six hours of sun a day is minimal. Never let the ground get too dry. Each stalk yields two to five ears, in 65 to 90 days, depending on the variety. Successive planting with corn is crucial; space the plantings about 3 weeks apart. Or you can plant varieties with different maturation dates. Corn does not store well, although freezing is acceptable, so plant for harvests to yield only what the family can consume immediately. Plant a special variety suitable for freezing. And remember, to ensure pollination, to plant at least four rows instead of one long one. Don't worry about the suckers at the base. They will not sap strength, and removing them may actually reduce the yield. Plant seeds 1½ inches deep 3 or 4 inches apart. Space rows 3 feet apart. Thin to the strongest seedling every 12 inches.

The Harvest There is only a 24-hour period when corn is at its harvest peak. The corn is ready when the silks at the ears turn brown and the ears feel full of juice. Pull back the husk if uncertain, and prick a kernel. If ready, it will produce a milky liquid; if immature, it will give water; if over-mature, it will be sticky. Set water to boil. Then go to pick the corn. Pull down the ear and twist. Pick all that is ready, cook it, and save the leftover cooked kernels for later.

The Basics
One 6-inch ear = 1 serving = ½ cup kernels.
One 6-inch ear cooked (3.5 ounces) = 100 calories = 21 grams carbohydrates, 3.3 grams protein.
10-foot row = about 40 ears (plant 4 rows of desired length at same time).

The Storage
Refrigeration storage is not advisable. Corn should be eaten immediately or frozen immediately for winter use. However, garden-grown corn stored in the refrigerator is still better than store-bought corn. An alternative to storing such a bulky product in the refrigerator is to put the stems in a pail of cold water to keep it from drying out before use.

Freezing
Frozen corn is not as sweet or crisp as fresh corn. Husk and silk. Trim ends. Freeze only excellent ears of corn. Freeze the small ones whole, and freeze the kernels only of the large ears. *For whole ears:* Scald 4 minutes. Chill in ice water. Drain. To avoid their sticking together, place ears on a cookie sheet, freeze, and wrap in plastic the instant they are frozen through. Label and quickly return to freezer. *To freeze kernels:*

Scald whole corn 4 minutes. Plunge in ice water. Drain. Cut off kernels and freeze in labeled packages of convenient size.

The Cooking Corn may be boiled or sautéed after husks and silks are removed. For roasting, leave husks on, or simply pull them back, but not off, to remove the silks, then rewrap around corn.

Basic Preparation *Corn on the cob:* Although roasted corn was the original cooking method, most Americans now boil it. Corn fresh from harvest requires only 3 or 4 minutes in boiling water. Never add salt to the water, as it hardens the kernels. Serve it with lots of butter, salt, and freshly ground pepper. Count on everybody's eating at least two ears. For variety serve corn on the cob with an herb butter (page 454). *Barbecued Corn on the Cob:* Brush corn with butter and season. Wrap in a dampened paper towel, and roll tightly in aluminum foil. Grill over coals for 20 minutes, turning frequently. *Creamed Fresh Corn:* Remove the kernels from uncooked corn by scoring each row with a paring knife. Make sure the skin is well cut. Then, with the back of a knife, press out kernels and corn milk. Cook over low heat 5 minutes. Stir in butter, salt, and freshly ground pepper.

CORN AND POTATO SOUP

6 slices bacon

Fry and crumble. Reserve 3 tablespoons bacon grease in skillet.

½ cup chopped onion

Sauté in bacon grease until soft.

2 tablespoons flour
1 teaspoon salt
1 teaspoon freshly ground pepper

Blend in.

3 cups milk
1 cup half-and-half
1 cup cooked and diced potatoes
1 cup cooked and diced carrots

Stir in. Cook until broth is thickened and smooth.

3 cups corn kernels, cooked or raw
Minced fresh parsley

Stir in corn and heat. For uncooked corn simmer 10 minutes. Stir in crumbled bacon. Serve topped with parsley.

Serves 4–6

CORN SALAD I

2½   cups cooked corn kernels
½   red or green pepper, diced
2   tomatoes, diced
2   green onions, minced
½   cup sliced green olives
½   cup diced celery

Combine.

¼   cup salad oil
¼   cup wine vinegar
¼   cup water
2   tablespoons taco seasoning

Combine and pour over salad. Stir to blend. Chill at least 2 hours before serving.

Serves 6

A natural for leftover corn.

Use same vegetables for preceding salad but substitute the following dressing.

CORN SALAD II

½ **cup sour cream**
½ **teaspoon Dijon mustard**
½ **teaspoon Worcestershire sauce**
1 **tablespoon vinegar**
    Salt and pepper to taste

Mix together and toss with vegetables. Chill and serve.

FRIED CORN KERNELS

6 strips bacon

Fry bacon. Remove and crumble. Leave 2 table-spoons grease in skillet.

1 onion, chopped
$1/_3$ cup green pepper

Cook until soft in bacon grease.

$1/_4$ cup water
2 cups corn cut from cob
1 teaspoon salt
1 teaspoon freshly ground pepper

Add to skillet, cover, and simmer 5 minutes. Remove cover. Boil away liquid. Stir in crumbled bacon.

Serves 4–6

Corn prepared in this manner offers a real challenge to our old standby, corn on the cob. Six-to-sixty-year-olds may appreciate the obvious advantage of corn off the cob.

CORN AND GREEN PEPPER HASH

  2 **tablespoons butter**
  1 **cup diced green peppers**
  1 **cup sliced mushrooms**

Sauté until soft.

  2 **cups cooked corn kernels**
  1 **tablespoon chopped chives**
  1 **tablespoon chopped fresh parsley**
     Salt and pepper to taste

Add. Stir to heat.

Serves 4

OLD-TIME CORN FRITTERS

2 cups fresh corn kernels
3 eggs, beaten
2 tablespoons milk
1 tablespoon melted butter
1 teaspoon baking powder
$^1/_2$ teaspoon salt
$^1/_8$ teaspoon pepper
$1^1/_4$ cups flour (approximately)

Mix together in order given, adding just enough flour to hold fritters together.

Oil for deep frying

Drop by tablespoons in hot oil and cook 3 to 5 minutes. Drain on paper towels.

Serves 6

This recipe dates from the Gold Rush days of California. Serve fritters warm with maple syrup.

BAKED CORN WITH CHEESE

    4   tablespoons butter
    4   tablespoons flour
1½   cups milk

Over medium heat stir together with whisk until sauce thickens. Remove from heat.

    2   cups fresh corn kernels
1½   cups grated cheddar cheese
    3   eggs, beaten
    1   tablespoon Dijon mustard
    ½   teaspoon sugar
    ¼   teaspoon salt
        Dash of pepper
    1   cup fresh bread crumbs

Add in order given. Bake in 2-quart buttered dish at 325° 1 hour, until center is firm.

Serves 4

ACAPULCO CORN

3 tablespoons butter
3 cups chopped onion

Sauté until soft in large skillet.

3 cups corn cut from the cob
¼ cup water

Add to skillet and cook 5 minutes over medium heat, stirring once. Remove cover and reduce liquid.

½ cup sour cream
**1 cup grated Monterey Jack or
    mozzarella cheese**
2 diced jalapeño chilis
¾ teaspoon salt
¾ teaspoon freshly ground pepper

Stir in, heating until cheese melts.

Serves 6

For leftover corn, simply sauté onions, toss all the ingredients in a gratin pan, and heat in the oven.

CORN AND TAMALE CASSEROLE

2   tablespoons butter
1   onion chopped
2   tablespoons chopped green pepper
2   green onions, chopped
1   stalk celery, chopped
    Salt and fresh ground pepper
        to taste

Sauté until soft.

1½ cups cooked corn kernels
1   16-ounce can tamales
    Chili powder (optional)

Layer half the sautéed vegetables, corn and tamales; repeat. Each layer may be sprinkled with chili powder. Bake at 350° for 20 minutes.

Serves 4

FARMER'S CORN PUDDING

>   2   tablespoons minced green pepper
>   2   tablespoons butter

Sauté in large skillet until soft.

>   2   cups creamed corn cut from cob
>   Dashes of white pepper and salt
>   ½   teaspoon sugar

Add to skillet.

>   2   egg yolks
>   2   whole eggs
>   ¼   cup milk

Combine and beat. Add slowly to corn off heat, stirring constantly.

>   2   egg whites, beaten stiff

Fold into corn. Pour into buttered dish and bake at 375° for 40 to 45 minutes.

Serves 4

Somewhat puffy, golden brown on top, and flecked through with green. Corn pudding is an American country version of soufflé.

CORN PANCAKES

2 cups cooked corn
1 egg, beaten
1 cup buttermilk
2 teaspoons bacon grease

Mix well.

½ cup flour
½ teaspoon baking soda
½ teaspoon salt
½ teaspoon sugar

Mix and stir into corn. Fry as pancakes on greased skillet.

Serves 4

Fantastic breakfast for leftover corn! Eat with syrup, and serve with bacon and sliced tomatoes.

SPOON BREAD

1½ cups milk

Scald milk.

¾ cup corn meal

Add, stirring constantly.

2 cups fresh corn kernels
3 tablespoons butter
1 teaspoon salt
1 teaspoon baking powder
4 egg yolks

Add, stirring so egg yolks blend in well.

4 egg whites, stiffly beaten

Fold in. Pour into buttered casserole or ring. Bake 30 minutes at 350°.

Serves 6

MEXICAN CORN BREAD

        3   cups corn meal
     2½   cups milk
        3   eggs, beaten
     1½   cups cooked corn kernels
     2–4 roasted and diced chili peppers
     2½   cups grated cheddar cheese
        1   large onion, grated
        ½   cup salad oil

Stir together in order given. Pour into hot 6-cup greased ring mold or Bundt pan and bake at 375° for 45 minutes. Unmold and serve hot.

Serves 6

Be sure to heat your mold in oven before adding batter. This ensures a shiny golden crust. Two table-spoons sugar can be substituted for the chili peppers for a sweet corn bread.

CORN RELISH

1 **green pepper, minced**
5 **stalks celery, sliced**

Parboil 5 minutes. Drain.

1 **Bermuda onion, chopped**
4 **cups cooked corn kernels**

Add to pepper and celery.

¼ **cup sugar**
1 **tablespoon salt**
1 **tablespoon mustard seed**
½ **cup white vinegar**
½ **cup water**

Bring to boil. Reduce to simmer. Add all vegetables. Simmer 15 minutes. Pour into sterilized jars. Seal. Or chill and use immediately.

4 pints

Real down-home cooking!

CUCUMBERS

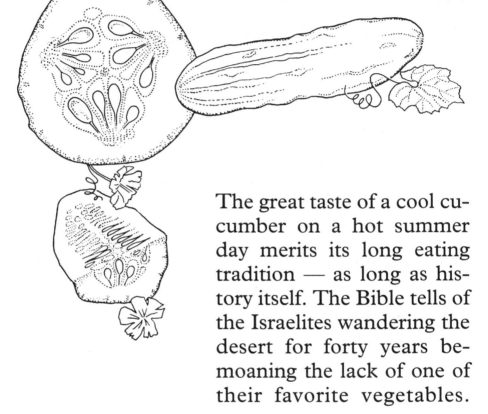

The great taste of a cool cucumber on a hot summer day merits its long eating tradition — as long as history itself. The Bible tells of the Israelites wandering the desert for forty years bemoaning the lack of one of their favorite vegetables.

The Romans always ate cucumbers in their salads, and the Chinese make reference to them as early as 140 B.C. The cucumbers known by these people were prickly and warted and curved to the shape of a quarter-moon.

Some insist on distinguishing between pickling and eating cucumbers; however, pickling cucumbers can be eaten raw, and eating ones can be pickled. It is mostly a matter of size: pickling cucumbers are generally small and eating cucumbers are large. Lemon cucumbers are an interesting variety; they look like lemons but are curiously sweeter and less acidic than ordinary cukes. English and Armenian are long and skinny, sometimes seedless. Japanese and Chinese cucumbers are even longer and skinnier.

The Growing Cucumbers, like kids, love summer and water. They grow on a vine and need hot days and warm nights (55°), although extreme heat may stop production. Cucumber vines have roots 3 feet deep. Water slowly and deeply. The cucumber is 95 percent water! The vine will stop growing from lack of water, but will start again as watered. Trellis vines for space control and better-looking straight fruit. Don't worry about planting near squash or melons (all members of the cucurbit family) as there is no chance of cross-pollination or bitterness. Cucumbers require 50 to 60 days from seed to harvest and will produce all summer. Cucumbers do not transplant well, so the seeds should be sown in the ground. Plant in rich soil in rows spaced 6 to 8 feet apart, placing seeds at 4-inch intervals or in groups of 6 to 8 seeds spaced at 4 to 6 inch intervals. Cover firmly with ½ inch of soil. Thin to 1 inch apart or 3 plants per group.

The Harvest Cucumbers have both male and female flowers. The males pollinate the females via the bees, and then the cucumber grows behind the female flower. An ordinary cucumber is ready to eat at 3 inches but is best at 5 inches. The young ones are bright green. As they age, they get darker in color. Keep vines well picked. One mature cucumber, which will be yellow, will stop production of the entire vine. Cut young cucumbers off rather than pulling, to avoid damage to the vine.

The Basics
1 pound = two 6-inch cucumbers = 3 cups sliced cucumbers = 4 servings.
One 5-inch cucumber (3.5 ounces) = 12–16 calories, 3 grams carbohydrates, 5 grams protein.
10-foot row = 10 plants = 30 pounds.

The Storage Wash off dirt. Dry. Store 1 to 2 weeks in plastic wrap in crisper drawer.

Freezing Cucumbers do not freeze well because of enormous water content.

The Cooking Cucumbers are primarily eaten raw. They are sliced thinly for marinating or for salad. The skin may be scored for effect. They do not need to be seeded. Small young cucumbers will have fewer and smaller seeds than commercial cucumbers.

Complementary Herbs Basil, chervil, chives, dill weed, mint, and parsley.

CUCUMBER CANAPÉS

Put cucumbers on spreads just before serving — they will cry and wilt if they sit around. Top with minced parsley or other fresh herb.

20 toast rounds

Arrange on serving platter.

20 slices cucumber

Soak in salted ice water, then drain and pat dry.

20 canapés

Blue Cheese Spread

3 tablespoons crumbled blue cheese
3 tablespoons butter
1 tablespoon lemon juice
Salt to taste

Cream together, spread on toast, and top with cucumber.

Paprika Spread

3 ounces cream cheese
1 tablespoon paprika

Mix until smooth, then spread on toast rounds. Top with cucumber.

Curried Shrimp Spread

½ cup very small or minced
   cooked shrimp
1½ tablespoons minced green onions
3 tablespoons mayonnaise
   Dash of Worcestershire sauce
½ teaspoon curry powder

Cream together, spread on toast, and top with cucumber.

CHICKEN AND CUCUMBER CANAPÉ

½ cup minced chicken
¼ cup minced cucumber
4 tablespoons mayonnaise,
   more for dry chicken
   Salt and pepper to taste
40 toast rounds
   Fresh chopped dill

Mix together. Spread mixture on toast rounds. Heat 5 minutes at 375°. Sprinkle with fresh chopped dill.

40 canapés

CUKE DIP

$^1/_2$ **cup finely chopped cucumber**
  8 **ounces cream cheese**
  2 **tablespoons sour cream**
$^1/_2$ **clove garlic, minced**
$^1/_8$ **teaspoon pepper**
  2 **teaspoons wine vinegar**
  2 **tablespoons fresh minced parsley**
  3 **tablespoons paprika**

Mix to blend well. Chill at least 2 hours.

$1^1/_2$ cups

This is a delightful pink dip flecked with green. Serve with corn chips, assorted vegetables, or chunks of French bread.

STUFFED CUCUMBER RINGS

2 cucumbers

Remove seeds and center with apple corer.

3 ounces cream cheese
1 tablespoon sour cream
¼ cup minced fresh parsley
¼ cup minced walnuts
¼ cup minced chives
1 teaspoon paprika
2 anchovies, minced (optional)
Freshly ground pepper to taste

Mix well and stuff into cucumber center. Chill until firm. Slice.

20 canapés

Serve as an hors d'oeuvre, or mound slices on lettuce and top with sour cream. Garnish with lemon wedges.

CUCUMBER SOUP

 3 **cups sliced cucumbers**
 ½ **onion, minced**
 2 **tablespoons butter**

Sauté in large skillet.

 1 **teaspoon salt**
 1 **tablespoon flour**
 2 **cups chicken broth**
   Juice of 1 lemon
   Pinch of dried dill weed

Add to skillet and simmer 10 minutes. Purée in blender and chill. (Freeze, if desired, at this point.)

 1 **cup sour cream**
 1 **cucumber, seeded and grated**

Stir in and serve cold.

Serves 4–6

MARINATED CUCUMBER SALAD

2 cucumbers, sliced paper-thin

Soak in salted ice water. Chill. Drain.

1 onion, thinly sliced
½ cup vinegar
¼ cup water
1 to 3 tablespoons sugar
1 teaspoon salt
Freshly ground pepper to taste

Mix well and combine with cucumbers to serve.

Serves 4

SALMON SALAD WITH CUCUMBER DRESSING

1 cup minced cucumbers

Drain for several hours.

½ teaspoon salt
1 tablespoon dried dill weed
1 cup sour cream

Mix with cucumber and chill.

1 head Romaine lettuce, torn
1½ cups salmon chunks, freshly cooked
    or canned
1½ cups thinly sliced celery
1½ cups crisply cooked broccoli chunks
1½ cups cherry tomatoes

Pour dressing over and toss lightly.

Serves 6–8

CUCUMBERS IN SOUR CREAM

   4 **medium cucumbers, thinly sliced**
1½ **teaspoons salt**
     Vinegar

Arrange slices in shallow bowl, sprinkle with salt, add vinegar to cover. Let stand 30 minutes. Drain well.

   1 **cup sour cream**
 ½ **teaspoon dried dill weed**
     Dash of pepper
     Diced red onion (optional)

Combine all and toss with cucumbers. Chill.

Serves 6–8

CUCUMBER RICE SALAD

1 clove garlic, mashed
¼ teaspoon salt
¼ teaspoon dry mustard
4 tablespoons red wine vinegar
3 tablespoons oil

Shake together in a jar.

6 cups hot cooked rice

Pour dressing over rice, adding as much dressing as can be absorbed. Let cool.

3 cucumbers, seeded, diced, and drained
½ cup chopped fresh mint
½ cup chopped walnuts
Salt and pepper to taste
Lemon juice to taste

Toss with rice. Chill.

Serves 6–8

Serve the salad very cold, sprinkled with finely chopped chives.

CHINESE CUCUMBER SALAD

3–4 six-inch cucumbers

Peel if you wish, cut lengthwise, and scrape out any large seeds. Slice ¼ inch thick. Soak in salted ice water 30 minutes. Drain.

4 tablespoons red wine vinegar
4 tablespoons soy sauce
4 tablespoons sugar
4 teaspoons sesame oil
2 teaspoons salt
1 teaspoon Tabasco

Mix and pour over cucumbers. Let stand 30 minutes prior to serving.

Serves 4

SHRIMP AND CUCUMBER
FRIED RICE

  2 **tablespoons oil**
  2 **cucumbers, peeled, seeded and**
      halved lengthwise, and cut into
      1-inch slices
 ½ **cup sliced celery**
 ½ **cup green pepper slices**

Sauté 3 to 5 minutes in large skillet.

  1 **pound shelled raw shrimp**
  2 **teaspoons salt**
  1 **teaspoon sugar**

Add to skillet and cook; stirring until shrimp turns pink.

  4 **tablespoons oil**
 ¼ **cup chopped onion**
 ¼ **cup sliced celery**

Stir-fry until crisp-tender in saucepan.

  4 **cups cooked rice**
  1 **tablespoon soy sauce**
  2 **eggs, beaten**

Add to saucepan, and stir over hot flame 2 to 3 minutes. Place in bowl and pour hot cucumber-shrimp mixture over top.

Serves 4

JAPANESE CUCUMBERS

10 medium cucumbers, thinly sliced
¼ cup butter

Sauté 5 minutes. Then cover and simmer 20 minutes.

½ cup light cream

Add and simmer uncovered 20 minutes or more until liquid thickens.

¼ teaspoon salt
Pepper and nutmeg to taste

Stir in and serve.

Serves 6

FRIED CUCUMBERS

3 small cucumbers

Slice ¼ inch thick.

¼ cup oil
¼ cup vinegar

Marinate cucumbers 10 minutes. Drain.

1 egg, beaten
Cracker crumbs

Dip in egg, then in crumbs.

Oil for deep frying

Fry in hot oil until golden brown. Drain. Serve immediately.

Serves 4

Don't marinate the cucumbers any longer than directed. The vinegar flavor should be subtle. Serve with sour cream and a sprinkle of fresh dill or parsley.

CUCUMBER SAUCE

1 **cucumber, seeded and finely chopped**
1 **green onion, chopped**
1 **tablespoon salt**

Mix and let sit at least 10 minutes. Drain.

1 **cup plain yogurt**
1 **tomato, seeded and chopped**
1 **tablespoon chopped fresh coriander or parsley**
1 **teaspoon cumin powder**

Add and chill.

1 pint

Make at least 1 hour before serving. This sauce is a refreshing side dish for curry along with peanuts, raisins, and coconut.

ICICLE PICKLES

12	small white onions
6	tablespoons celery seed
6	tablespoons mustard seed
30–35	small cucumbers (3 pounds or more)

Slice ½ onion into the bottom of each of 6 sterilized pint jars. Add 1 tablespoon celery seed and 1 tablespoon mustard seed to each. Slice cucumbers very thin lengthwise and stand up in jars as tightly as possible. Slice remaining onions on top of each.

1	quart vinegar
1	cup sugar
	Scant ¼ cup salt

Boil 2 minutes. Pour over cucumbers and seal jars.

6 pints

HELEN'S BREAD-AND-BUTTER PICKLES

12 large unpeeled pickling cucumbers
6 medium onions, peeled
Salt

Slice and sprinkle heavily with salt. Let stand overnight, then drain.

4 cups vinegar
4 cups sugar
2 teaspoons celery seed
2 teaspoons mustard seed
2 teaspoons ground ginger
½–1 teaspoon turmeric

Bring to boil. Add onion and cucumbers and return to hard boil. Pack at once in hot sterilized jars and seal.

6 pints

The very best!

HIGH-SOCIETY
SWEET PICKLE CHIPS

14 large pickling cucumbers

Cover with boiling water. Let stand 24 hours. Drain, and repeat process daily for 3 more days.

4 cups white vinegar
6 cups sugar
5 tablespoons mixed pickling spices
1 tablespoon salt

On the fifth day, slice cucumbers ¼ inch thick. Bring rest of ingredients to a boil and pour over cucumbers. Let stand 24 hours. Drain and reheat syrup. Again pour over slices. Repeat one more day. On the eighth day, drain syrup and heat to boiling. Add cucumber slices and return to boiling. Pack in sterilized jars. Seal.

8 pints

Also known as 8-day pickles.

EGGPLANT

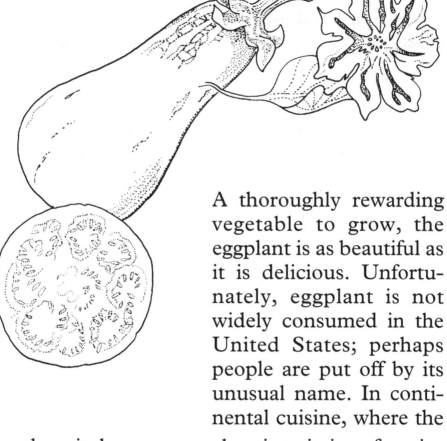

A thoroughly rewarding vegetable to grow, the eggplant is as beautiful as it is delicious. Unfortunately, eggplant is not widely consumed in the United States; perhaps people are put off by its unusual name. In continental cuisine, where the eggplant is known as aubergine, it is a favorite choice for spectacular vegetable dishes. The eggplant, a member of the tomato and potato family, is believed to be native to China and India. The Europeans of the Middle Ages grew eggplants of many colors. Current varieties include the familiar egg-shaped purple eggplants, long cylindrical purple ones (Japanese), and white ones.

Many people erroneously think of eggplant as a meat substitute. Although the eggplant is high in carbohydrates, it has only a fraction of the protein content of meat.

The Growing Eggplant is a warm-weather lover. A 55° night and 80° day are its minimum tolerance. It requires 4 months to grow from seed, 60 to 75 days from transplanted seedlings. Since eggplant needs warm nights, it is best to germinate the seeds early indoors in peat pots. Plant 2 seeds 1½ inches deep per pot. Thin to one strong plant. Keep plants warm and moist. When nights are 55° or above, transplant at 2½-foot intervals in rows spaced 3 feet apart. The long, stable summer requirements are why this vegetable is common to the hot Mediterranean cuisine. The plant grows 2 to 3 feet tall in normal summer climates, but in the tropics it may reach a height of 8 feet. Water by soaking; the fruit needs a constant source of deep water. The varieties with large fruit may need staking.

The Harvest Large eggplants may reach a maximum length of 10 inches, but they are vastly superior at the half-grown stage, 4 to 6 inches. These baby eggplants justify the efforts of any gardener. A good eggplant has high gloss; dull color indicates overripe fruit. To test ripeness, push on the fruit with thumb; it should not spring back. Be sure to pick the fruit before it reaches maturation or the plant will stop producing. Brown seeds inside the eggplant indicate maturation and that the eggplant is no longer fit to eat.

The Basics
1 pound = 1 large eggplant = 3–3½ cups cooked = 4 servings.
½ cup diced cooked eggplant (3.5 ounces) = 19 calories; 4.1 grams carbohydrates; 1 gram protein (55-60 grams daily recommended).
10-foot row = 4 plants = 20–40 eggplants.

The Storage Eggplant stores one week in the refrigerator. It need not be wrapped.

Freezing Because of its high water content, raw eggplant does not freeze very well. Freeze in slices or cubes. Peel and slice ¼ inch thick, or cut in cubes. Drop pieces into cold, salted water to maintain pure color. Scald 4½ minutes for slices, 3 minutes for cubes. Chill in water. Drain. Layer on sheets of wax paper on cookie sheet and place in freezer. As soon as frozen remove and place in labeled plastic sacks of convenient size. Eggplant purée is also satisfactorily frozen, and it is excellent for a number of casseroles. To prepare, peel and dice eggplant. Drop pieces in cold, salted water. Scald 10 to 15 minutes. Drain. Purée in blender. Package in plastic sacks of convenient size. Label. A casserole itself may be frozen, but it should not be thawed before heating.

The Cooking Young, very fresh eggplant does

not need to be peeled. However, if desired, peel it carefully with a paring knife or a potato peeler. Many recipes relying on sliced eggplant require a period of salting to withdraw some excess water and prevent the dish from being watery and mushy. It may be boiled in slices or pieces, baked whole or half, or fried. It is rather bland and not usually served plain. Tomatoes, onions, and olive oil add depth and complexity to the eggplant flavor. A good plain eggplant preparation is to fry it breaded and serve with lemon wedges.

Complementary Herbs Basil, chili powder, oregano, and sage.

EGGPLANT MINESTRONE

2 tablespoons olive oil
1 large onion, chopped
1 pound lean ground beef
2 cloves garlic, minced

Sauté 5 minutes in large soup kettle.

1 medium-sized eggplant,
   peeled and diced

Stir into kettle and cook 3 minutes.

3 zucchini, diced
3 carrots, diced
2 stalks celery, diced
8 large tomatoes, peeled and quartered
4 cups beef stock
1 teaspoon dried oregano
1 teaspoon dried basil
1 teaspoon salt
1 teaspoon sugar

Add to kettle and simmer uncovered 1 to 2 hours.

½ cup elbow macaroni
¼ teaspoon pepper

Add and cook 20 minutes.

Serves 8

A hearty Italian soup. Sprinkle with freshly grated Parmesan cheese.

EGGPLANT CAVIAR

1 large eggplant

Bake at 400° for 1 hour. Peel and chop.

½ cup olive oil
½ large onion, minced
1 green pepper, chopped
1 clove garlic, crushed

Sauté until vegetables are soft in large skillet.

½ teaspoon salt
Pepper to taste
2 tablespoons white wine
1 tablespoon lemon juice

Add to skillet, stir in eggplant, and simmer about 15 minutes, until mixture is thick. Chill.

Serves 8

It's always nice to find a dip that's not the same old fattening sour cream approach. Serve with large corn chips.

BAKED EGGPLANT SLICES

**1 medium eggplant, peeled
     and sliced ½ inch thick
Salt**

Sprinkle with salt, let stand 20 minutes, then pat dry.

**½ cup mayonnaise
½ green onion, finely minced**

Mix and spread on both sides of eggplant.

**1 cup soda cracker crumbs
½ cup grated Parmesan cheese**

Mix. Dip slices into mixture. Place on cookie sheet and bake at 375° until golden, about 20 minutes.

Serves 4

PICNIC SALAD

2 small eggplants, peeled and cubed
½ cup olive oil

Sauté 10 to 15 minutes, until soft.

1 Bermuda onion, cut in small chunks
1½ cups chunked celery
1 cup chunked green pepper
1 cup pitted black olives
1½ cups bottled chili sauce
1 teaspoon salt
Freshly ground pepper to taste
½ cup red wine vinegar
¼ cup water

Mix and marinate overnight.

Serves 8

Chunks of red, green, black, and white in a spicy tomato sauce blend well with most any meal. Spectacular in a glass bowl! Serve with French bread and sweet butter.

FRIED EGGPLANT

1 eggplant, peeled
Salt

Slice ¾ inch thick, sprinkle with salt, and let stand 20 to 30 minutes. Wipe dry. Squeeze out excess moisture.

2 beaten eggs
Cracker crumbs

Dip slices in egg, then in crumbs. Refrigerate 30 minutes to dry.

½ cup oil

Fry in oil until golden brown. Drain and serve.

Serves 4–6

RATATOUILLE

    2   onions, chopped
  2–3   cloves garlic, minced
    ¼   cup oil

Sauté until soft in Dutch oven.

    ¼   cup oil
    2   medium eggplants, sliced in strips
  6–8   zucchini, sliced

Add and cook 5 minutes, stirring frequently.

    4   tomatoes, peeled and chopped
    2   green peppers, chopped
    2   teaspoons salt
    ½   teaspoon dried thyme
         Freshly ground pepper to taste
    2   leaves fresh basil, chopped

Add to pot, cover, and simmer over low heat 1 hour. Stir often.

Serves 6

A classic dish from southern France. Combine with favorite summer vegetables. Leave on the purple eggplant skin for a show of color.

TOMATO-TOPPED EGGPLANT

1 eggplant, cut in 6 slices
Olive oil
Salt and pepper to taste

Brush slices with oil. Broil each side 3 minutes. Season.

6 slices tomato
1 cup grated white cheese
6 slices bacon, cooked and crumbled

Top in order given. Bake at 350° about 20 minutes.

Serves 6

A good choice for frozen eggplant slices. Assemble with frozen slices, and increase baking time.

EGGPLANT FRITTERS

  2 **medium eggplants, peeled**
  1 **tablespoon salt**

Cut eggplants into fingers. Toss with salt. Let stand 20 minutes. Drain and dry.

  1 **cup flour**
  1 **teaspoon baking powder**
$^1/_2$ **teaspoon salt**
    Dash of pepper
  2 **eggs, beaten**
$^2/_3$ **cup cold milk**
  1 **tablespoon salad oil**

Mix to make batter. Dip eggplant in batter.

    Oil for deep frying
    Lemon wedges

Drop eggplant fingers into hot oil a few at a time. Drain and serve with lemon wedges.

Serves 6–8

STUFFED EGGPLANT

1 large eggplant or 2 medium
    eggplants
Juice of ½ lemon

Halve and parboil 15 minutes. Drain. Scoop out meat and mash. Reserve shells.

1 chopped onion
½ pound cheddar cheese, grated
2 eggs, well beaten
1 cup fine, dry bread crumbs
½ cup milk
Salt, pepper, dried basil to taste

Mix with mashed eggplant. Stuff shells. Bake at 350° for 30 minutes, until bubbly.

Serves 4

It seems wasteful that the natural beauty of eggplant is not displayed more. Here it is as a real eye-pleaser — a puffy cheese mixture in eggplant shells.

MEXICAN EGGPLANT

1   medium eggplant, peeled, cubed, parboiled, and drained
2–3   bread slices, soaked in milk and squeezed dry
1   cup sliced black olives
1   cup tomato sauce
1½   teaspoons chili powder
¼   teaspoon salt
2   cups corn kernels
2   eggs, beaten
2   cups grated cheddar cheese

Mix together, reserving half of the cheese. Pour into greased casserole. Top with remaining cheese. Bake at 350° for 35 to 45 minutes, until puffy.

Serves 4

INDIA EGGPLANT

½   **cup olive oil**
3   **cloves garlic, mashed**
1   **onion, chopped**
1   **green pepper, chopped**
1   **teaspoon powdered coriander**
1   **teaspoon turmeric**
1   **teaspoon cumin**
1   **teaspoon powdered ginger**

Cook slowly 10 minutes until onion is translucent.

1   **medium eggplant, cut in ¾-inch cubes**
3–4   **tomatoes, chopped**
1   **tablespoon brown sugar**

Add, and place in buttered casserole. Cook 1 hour at 375°.

Serves 3–4

Nice and spicy. Leftover lamb could be tossed in for the last 20 minutes.

RATATOUILLE PIZZA

$^1/_3$ **cup olive oil**
2 **cloves garlic, minced**

Cook together 2 minutes in large skillet.

4 **large ripe tomatoes**

Cut tomatoes in 2-inch chunks, add to skillet, and sauté until soft.

2 **medium zucchini**
2 **onions**
2 **green peppers**
1 **medium eggplant, peeled**
2 **teaspoons salt**
   Dash of pepper
$^1/_2$ **teaspoon dried oregano**
$^1/_2$ **teaspoon dried thyme**

Cut all vegetables in 2-inch pieces. Add to skillet with seasonings. Simmer uncovered about 1½ hours, stirring occasionally, until puréed and almost dry.

$^2/_3$ **cup butter**
6 **ounces cream cheese**
$^1/_2$ **teaspoon salt**
2–3 **cups unsifted flour**
   Melted butter

Cream butter, cream cheese and salt. Add flour until dough forms a firm ball. Chill 1 hour to 2

days. Roll out to fit cookie sheet. Bake at 375°
for 12 minutes. Glaze with melted butter.

½ cup grated Parmesan cheese

Spread vegetable purée across crust. Sprinkle
with cheese. Broil about 4 minutes.

Serves 8

*Very nice for lunch; something like a sandwich. It's
just as good cold or reheated.*

EGGPLANT PARMIGIANA

2 medium eggplants, unpeeled
¼ cup flour
  Olive oil

Slice ½ inch thick, dip in flour, and fry in oil over high heat until soft.

2 tablespoons olive oil
2 cloves garlic, minced
6 tomatoes, peeled and chopped
1 stalk celery, minced
1 tablespoon minced fresh parsley
2 carrots, minced
1 tablespoon chopped fresh basil
1 onion, minced
¼ teaspoon salt
¼ teaspoon sugar
¼ teaspoon pepper

Mix and cook 30 minutes.

½ cup red wine

Add and continue simmering until sauce thickens.

½ cup grated Parmesan cheese
1 pound Gruyère or mozzarella cheese, sliced thinly

In greased dish, layer eggplant, sauce, then cheeses on top. Bake at 350° for 30 to 40 minutes before serving.

Serves 6

EGGPLANT WITH PORK
AND GARLIC

2 tablespoons soy sauce
2 tablespoons dry sherry
2 teaspoons cornstarch
2 teaspoons sugar

Mix.

1 pound pork chops
2 tablespoons peanut oil

Cut pork into slivers, about 2 inches long and $^1/_8$ inch thick. Toss in soy sauce mixture. Stir-fry in oil until done. Remove.

1 large green pepper
1 large red sweet pepper
1–2 tablespoons peanut oil

Cut peppers into slivers same size as pork. Stir-fry until limp. Remove.

1 large eggplant
  Salt
10 cloves garlic, mashed
2 tablespoons (or more) peanut oil

Cut eggplant into pieces about 2 inches long and $^1/_2$ inch thick. Sprinkle with salt and let stand 20 minutes. Squeeze dry. Brown in oil with garlic.

$^1/_2$ cup water
1 tablespoon soy sauce

1 tablespoon sherry
1 teaspoon sugar

Add to eggplant. Cover and cook about 10 minutes until liquid is absorbed or eggplant is done. Add pork and peppers. Heat.

Serves 2–3

To ensure even and fast cooking, the pork, peppers, and eggplant must be slivered into uniform sizes. For an exceptional summer dinner straight from the garden, serve with rice, Chinese cucumber salad (page 190), and a light fruit dessert.

MOUSSAKA

  1 **pound ground chuck**
  1 **small onion, chopped**
 ¼ **teaspoon cinnamon**
 ¼ **teaspoon nutmeg**
    Salt and pepper to taste
2–3 **tomatoes, peeled, seeded, and diced**
½–¾ **cup red wine**

Fry beef, mashing out lumps with a spoon. Sauté onion when grease appears. Add seasonings. When beef loses its color, add tomatoes and wine. Cover and cook 20 minutes. Break up tomatoes.

  1 **large eggplant, diced**
    Olive oil
  2 **medium zucchini, sliced**

Sauté eggplant in oil. Cover and cook 15 minutes. Add zucchini and cook until just tender.

 ¾ **cup freshly grated Romano cheese**
  4 **tablespoons freshly chopped parsley**

In a deep, oiled baking dish place a third of the eggplant-zucchini mixture. Add half the meat mixture, then half the cheese, then half the parsley. Repeat with remaining vegetables on top.

  3 **tablespoons butter**
1½ **tablespoons flour**
  1 **cup milk**
  3 **eggs, beaten**

Melt butter, stir in flour and cook, stirring, for several minutes. Stir in milk. Add eggs, stirring until thickened. Pour over casserole. Bake at 325° for 45 minutes to 1 hour.

Serves 4–5

STUFFED EGGPLANT
WITH MINTED LAMB

2 medium eggplants, halved

Scoop out pulp with melon baller, leaving shell ¾ inch thick. Do not puncture. Chop pulp.

¾-1 pound ground lamb

Fry lamb until some fat appears. Add eggplant pulp. Continue cooking until lamb is light brown.

2 cups tomato sauce
1½-2 tablespoons chopped fresh mint
1 teaspoon dried basil
½ teaspoon dried rosemary
Salt to taste

Add and simmer 10 minutes. Fill eggplant shells with mixture. Place in shallow greased pan and cover with foil. Bake 40 minutes, in 400° oven.

Serves 4

The mint makes the difference! Serve with fruit salad and rice pilaf.

LETTUCE

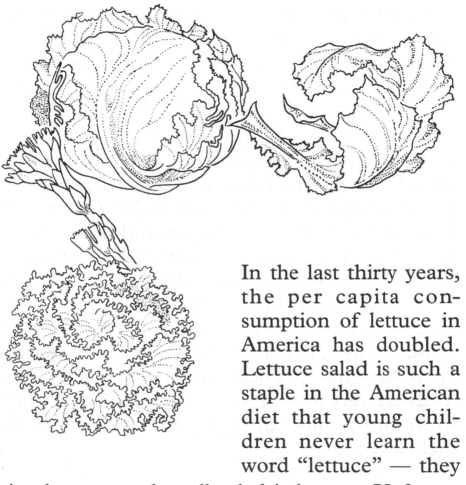

In the last thirty years, the per capita consumption of lettuce in America has doubled. Lettuce salad is such a staple in the American diet that young children never learn the word "lettuce" — they simply assume that all salad is lettuce. Unfortunately, many climates are not very hospitable to this leafy plant.

Four types of lettuce are grown in the United States. Crisphead lettuce, iceberg, leads the nation in popularity. Strangely enough, it is the most particular about weather. Too much heat, and crisphead lettuce will not head. This type matures

221

in 80 to 90 days from seed. Butterhead is a softer-leafed, gently headed form of lettuce. Bibb lettuce is the common variety of butterhead. Limestone lettuce is Bibb grown in limestone soil. Butterhead matures in about 75 days. Looseleaf lettuce, which includes many varieties, does not head. The leaves of looseleaf are very tender, especially when young. They are suitable for wilted salads. Familiar forms include the light-green Black-seeded Simpson, the deeply lobed Oak Leaf, and the red-shaded Ruby or Red Leaf. Looseleaf requires only 40 to 45 days to mature. Romaine or cos lettuce grows in a V shape rather than a ball. The leaves are coarser, crisper, and have a more distinct flavor. Cos lettuce is the hardiest variety, and will tolerate more heat without going to seed. It requires about 80 days from seed.

Endive, or chicory, and escarole belong to the same family, the chicory family, and are not related to lettuce. Their flavor is slightly bitter. They are very tolerant of cold and require 90 days to finish heading, although outer leaves may be picked sooner.

The Growing Lettuce requires temperatures ranging between 35° and 80°. Therefore, in most climates it is a spring/fall crop. In summer climates that peak at 90°, partial shade will permit all but iceberg to grow. Water is essential, as each leaf contains a great deal. If lettuce is allowed to get dry and wilt, it may never recover.

Sow seeds in the ground unless suitable climate

is so short that indoor germination would be beneficial. Scatter seeds thinly. Space rows 15 inches to 18 inches apart. Thin seedlings to 8 inches for all heading forms and 4 inches for looseleaf. The early thinnings may be transplanted, and the later ones used in salads. Protect young seedlings from birds with chicken wire.

The Harvest The outer leaves may be harvested as the plant is growing, particularly in the case of Romaine and looseleaf lettuce. The outer leaves have the most vitamins and minerals. To harvest the head, pull plant from the ground and cut off roots. Sometimes Romaine and looseleaf will sprout some leaves again if all leaves are cut off at the base.

The Basics
1 pound = 1 medium head = 3½ cups torn = 4 servings.
1 cup torn lettuce = 3.5 ounces = 14–18 calories, 2.3–3.5 grams carbohydrates, 1.2–1.3 grams protein, up to half daily recommended vitamin A, up to a third daily recommended vitamin C.
10-foot row = 12 heads (18 looseleaf).

The Storage *Iceberg:* Core. Wash thoroughly. Drain, core down. Store refrigerated in a plastic sack 1 week. *Butterhead and loose leaf:* Rinse. Shake off water. Store refrigerated 2 to 3 days in plastic sacks with a few paper towels to absorb moisture. Wash and dry each leaf before serving.

Romaine: Rinse whole. Refrigerate in plastic sack with paper towels for one week. Separate leaves, wash, and dry for serving.

The Cooking Lettuce is best raw in salads, although it can be braised. An excellent salad requires very cool, crisp, clean, and dry lettuce. The oil in the dressing will adhere well only to dry leaves. To dry, pat each leaf with a towel or dry in a lettuce dryer. Lettuce dryers may be simple — a basket with handles to sling off water — or sophisticated — hand-cranked or electric spinning baskets. To ensure that oil adheres well, add it first and separately to the lettuce. Toss, then add remaining ingredients. Toss again.

Complementary Herbs Basil, chives, dill weed, garlic, mint, mustard seed, oregano, parsley, and tarragon.

BASIC VINAIGRETTE

$^1/_3$ cup wine vinegar
1 cup olive or vegetable oil
$^1/_4$ teaspoon salt
$^1/_8$ teaspoon pepper

Combine in a jar. Cover and shake. Let stand.

$1^1/_3$ cups

VARIATIONS

Add 1–2 cloves of minced garlic or 2 tablespoons minced green onions.

Add 1–2 minced tablespoons of your favorite herb.

Add 1 tablespoon Dijon mustard.

CREAMY FRENCH DRESSING

2 cups salad oil
$1/2$ cup vinegar
3 tablespoons ketchup
2 tablespoons brown sugar
2 teaspoons grated onion
1 teaspoon paprika
1 teaspoon salt
$1/2$ egg white, beaten
$1/8$ teaspoon dry mustard
2 cloves garlic, peeled and halved

Combine all in a jar. Store in refrigerator.

THOUSAND-ISLAND DRESSING

1 cup mayonnaise
$1/4$ cup chili sauce
1 teaspoon grated onion
1 tablespoon sweet pickle relish
1 tablespoon chopped stuffed olives
2 hard-cooked eggs, minced
$1/4$ teaspoon Worcestershire sauce

Combine and chill so flavors blend.

HERB SALAD DRESSING

   2 **green onions, chopped**
   1 **clove garlic**
   1 **teaspoon salt**
 $^3/_4$ **teaspoon dried dill weed**
 $^1/_2$ **teaspoon dry mustard**
 $^1/_2$ **teaspoon paprika**
 $^1/_4$ **teaspoon dried tarragon**
 $^1/_4$ **teaspoon pepper**
   1 **tablespoon white vinegar**

Place in blender.

 $^1/_3$ **cup oil**

Blend in 1 tablespoon oil, then, with blender at low speed, add remaining oil in a slow stream.

   1 **cup plain yogurt**
 $^1/_4$-$^1/_2$ **cup buttermilk**

Blend in yogurt, adding buttermilk until desired thickness is reached. Store in covered jar and refrigerate up to 1 week.

Great for the dieter. No one will ever guess that the base is yogurt and buttermilk. Pour over wedges of head lettuce or on tossed greens.

FRENCH DRESSING WITH MINT

    1   cup olive oil
   ¾   cup red wine
    1   clove garlic, peeled
   ¼   teaspoon oregano
    1   tablespoon chopped fresh mint
       Salt and pepper to taste

Shake all together in a jar and let stand overnight if possible. Keeps for weeks in the refrigerator.

GREEN GODDESS DRESSING

    6   tablespoons tarragon vinegar
   ¼   cup chopped onion
   ¼   cup chopped fresh parsley
    1   cup mayonnaise
    1   cup sour cream
 1½   teaspoons anchovy paste
   ½   clove garlic, minced

Purée in blender. Chill.

3 cups

POPPY SEED DRESSING

$^1/_4$ **cup cider vinegar**
$^1/_2$ **cup sugar**
$^1/_2$ **teaspoon salt**
$^1/_8$ **teaspoon dry mustard**

Heat to boiling. Let cool.

1 **cup oil**

Slowly add oil while beating constantly with electric beater.

2 **teaspoons grated onion**
2 **teaspoons poppy seeds**

Stir in. Refrigerate for up to 2 weeks.

2 cups

Mound fresh fruits atop assorted salad greens and drizzle with this sweet dressing.

LETTUCE SOUP

4 cups finely chopped Romaine lettuce
1 cup water

Simmer covered 10 to 15 minutes, until tender.

2 tablespoons chopped onion
1 tablespoon butter
2½ cups chicken stock
½ cup light cream

Add and simmer 10 to 15 minutes.

Nutmeg
Salt and pepper

Season to taste.

Serves 6

Serve hot with browned, buttered croutons. Also good cold.

BUTTER LETTUCE SALAD

1 large head butter lettuce, torn
1 cup snow pea pods, parboiled and
   drained
½ cup sliced water chestnuts

Mix and chill.

3 tablespoons oil
1 tablespoon lemon juice
1 clove garlic, mashed
¼ teaspoon salt
¼ teaspoon pepper

Combine and let stand at room temperature. Toss with salad just before serving.

Serves 4–6

Add mandarin orange segments and sprinkle with toasted sesame seeds if you like.

COBB SALAD

½ cup salad oil
2 tablespoons olive oil
2 tablespoons red wine vinegar
2 tablespoons water
2 teaspoons lemon juice
¼ teaspoon salt
½ teaspoon Worcestershire sauce
½ teaspoon Dijon mustard
½ teaspoon pepper
½ small clove garlic, minced

Purée in blender, cover, and chill.

½ head Romaine lettuce
½ head iceberg lettuce
1 bunch watercress
1 small bunch chicory

Tear into bite-sized pieces and chill in large bowl.

3 tomatoes, peeled, seeded, and
      chopped
2 cups slivered cooked chicken
8 slices bacon, cooked and crumbled
1 avocado, sliced

In order given, arrange all on greens.

2 hard-boiled eggs, chopped
3 tablespoons chopped chives
½ cup crumbled Roquefort cheese

Sprinkle atop greens. Toss with about 1 cup dressing.

Serves 4–6

CAESAR SALAD

¾ cup oil
1 clove garlic, minced

Mix and let stand 4 hours to make garlic oil.

¼ cup garlic oil (above)
2 cups French bread cubes

Sauté bread cubes until browned. Drain on paper towels.

2 large heads Romaine lettuce
½ cup garlic oil (above)
½ teaspoon salt
1 teaspoon freshly ground pepper

Tear Romaine. Toss with oil. Add salt and pepper. Toss again.

1 egg, boiled 1 minute
1 large lemon

Break egg in salad. Squeeze lemon juice over salad. Toss.

6 anchovy fillets, diced
½ cup freshly grated Parmesan cheese

Add with reserved croutons. Toss again, and serve.

Serves 6

Several California chefs and restaurants claim to have invented this famous salad. It should be assembled and tossed at the table.

WILTED LETTUCE

6 slices bacon

Fry and crumble, reserving 4 tablespoons grease.

4 tablespoons vinegar
1 tablespoon sugar
¼ teaspoon salt
3 tablespoons minced green onion
Dash of pepper

Combine with bacon grease and heat.

1 head lettuce, torn apart

Pour hot dressing over lettuce, add bacon, and toss.

Serves 4–6

WON TON SALAD

4–5 cooked chicken breast halves

Bone and sliver.

2 tablespoons vegetable oil
1 tablespoon sesame oil
6 tablespoons sugar
8 tablespoons cider vinegar
1 teaspoon salt

Mix together and pour over chicken. Let stand at least 3 hours.

½ head lettuce, finely slivered
3 celery stalks, sliced on diagonal
5 green onions, sliced on diagonal
24 won ton skins, cut in strips and
    deep fried

Toss with chicken and serve.

Serves 4–6

TACO SALAD

1   pound lean ground beef
1   onion, chopped
1   tablespoon oil

Sauté and drain.

15-ounce can kidney beans, drained

Add to beef and simmer 10 minutes; let cool.

  1   head lettuce, torn
1–2   cups grated cheddar cheese
  4   tomatoes, chopped
  1   large avocado, sliced
    6-ounce package tortilla chips

Combine in large salad bowl with meat and beans.

French or Thousand Island dressing (p. 226)

Toss and serve.

Serves 6

Super for a family supper.

CHEF'S SALAD

$3/4$ **cup vegetable oil**
3   **cloves garlic, crushed**
    Juice of 1 large lemon
$1/4$ **teaspoon salt**
$1/4$ **teaspoon freshly ground pepper**
$1/3$ **cup grated Parmesan cheese**

Combine in a jar. Cover and shake. Let stand 4–6 hours.

2   **heads Romaine lettuce, torn**
$1^1/_2$ **cups cherry tomatoes**
1   **cup finely diced Swiss cheese**
1   **cup slivered and toasted almonds**
$1/4$ **pound bacon, cooked and crumbled**
$1/2$ **cup fresh croutons**

Toss with dressing. Serve immediately.

Serves 8

Slivered ham may be added or substituted for bacon.

SALADE NIÇOISE

12 small new potatoes
2 cups green beans, cut up

Cook separately in boiling water to cover until just tender. Drain, peel, and cut up the potatoes.

1 cup Basic Vinaigrette (p. 225)
1 tablespoon Dijon mustard
2 tablespoons heavy cream

While vegetables are warm, toss with enough dressing to coat (about ½ cup).

2 medium heads Boston lettuce

Arrange lettuce on chilled plates.

4 hard-boiled eggs, peeled and cut in
   wedges
3 tomatoes, cut in wedges
2 6½-ounce cans tuna chunks, drained
8 anchovy fillets, drained
1 tablespoon capers
½ cup pitted black olives
   Minced fresh parsley

Divide and arrange potatoes, beans, and rest of ingredients on the lettuce. Pour over rest of dressing and sprinkle with parsley.

Serves 4

High-quality tuna and garden-fresh vegetables are essential.

ONIONS

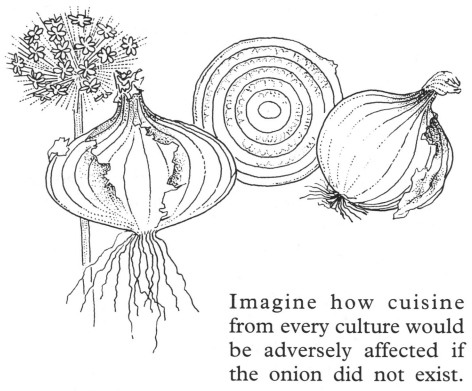

Imagine how cuisine from every culture would be adversely affected if the onion did not exist.

Onions are the most universal of all vegetable flavors. Countless dishes would be flat and lack distinction without the ever-present onion. Man has been eating onions, a member of the lily family, since before the birth of civilization. They are mentioned in Homer and in the Bible. In the Middle Ages onions were an integral part of the medicinal folklore. They were brought to the New World by Spanish explorers.

The onion family is extensive, encompassing many relatives and varieties. The most strongly flavored form is the globular onion. This may be yellow, white or red. Red onions have a sweet flavor, and are a good choice for salads and other dishes calling for raw onions. The pungent yellow and white onions are used primarily chopped, for flavoring in baked and sautéed dishes. Pearl and boiling onions are not a special variety; they are simply white onions harvested while still small. Green onions are the immature bulb of any onion variety.

Bunching onions, or scallions, are a mild-flavored, thick-stemmed relative of the onion, that does not form bulbs. They continue to divide at the base. They are good raw in salads, and an important ingredient in many Chinese stir-fry dishes. Leeks, like scallions, do not form bulbs and taste like a mild onion. Leeks are planted by seed, and blanched white during their 4-month growth period by mounding soil around the stem. Leeks are a prime ingredient in the famous cold potato soup, Vichyssoise. Garlic and shallots are included among the onion relatives. They are normally considered to be a flavoring ingredient rather than a vegetable.

The Growing Globe onions require 95 to 120 days to mature from seed; depending on variety and how large you want to let them grow. Most gardeners plant seedlings or small bulbs, called onion sets, which mature much faster. Onion sets are the tiny bulbs from last year's seedlings, retarded in growth. Onions prefer warm summer weather, and they grow best in rich, loose soil.

Each variety has somewhat varying daylight and temperature requirements. Plant an onion compatible with the area climate.

The Harvest When leaves start to turn yellow, bend stems (you can knock them over with your foot) level with the ground. This stops the top growth, diverting food energy to the bulb. Dig away some of the ground around the top to encourage the ripening process. Lift onions out when the leaves turn brown. Cut the leaves to 1 inch, and leave the onion to dry in the sun for a week. Or, leave onion leaves long, braid the tops, and hang to dry.

The Basics
1 pound = 4 two-inch globe onions = 2 cups chopped.
1 large raw onion (3.5 ounces) = 38 calories = 8.7 grams carbohydrates, 1.5 grams protein, and some vitamin C.
10-foot row = 10 pounds.

The Storage Store onions unwashed in a dark, cool, and very dry place. Excess moisture causes sprouting. They may be stored up to 3 months — or even longer under good conditions. Yellow onions store the longest. (The stronger the flavor, the longer the storage.) Green onions or scallions will store up to 2 weeks in a plastic sack in the refrigerator.

Freezing Chopped raw onions may be frozen in small bags of convenient size. They lack texture when thawed, but they are sometimes handy. And this is a good way to save onions that have begun to sprout.

The Cooking Onions should always be peeled. Cut off stem and slice off core at bottom. Remove dry outer skins. Then slice or chop. An easy way to chop is to slice thinly, stack slices and slice crosswise. To prevent crying, hold a couple of unlit matches, sulfur end out, in your mouth. The sulfur absorbs the irritating fumes. Or breathe through your mouth as you chop.

Basic Preparation To cook whole onions, cut an X in the bottom to keep onions from separating, cover with lightly salted boiling water and simmer 20 to 30 minutes. Drain.

Complementary Herbs Chili powder, chives, curry, garlic, mint, nutmeg, parsley, rosemary, tarragon.

LEEK AND VEGETABLE SOUP

1 small onion, chopped
2 tablespoons butter

Sauté in a large kettle for 5 minutes.

6 leeks, white part only

Cut each leek into four lengthwise slices. Wash under running water to remove any sand or dirt. Add to kettle and sauté 3 minutes.

3 cups peeled and diced potatoes
8 cups water
2 teaspoons salt

Add to kettle and boil slowly for about 45 minutes, until potatoes are tender and breaking apart. Crush potatoes with a wooden spoon or potato masher.

1 cup shredded cabbage
1 cup peas, diced beans, or summer squash

Add to the kettle and simmer 15 minutes.

1 tomato, peeled, seeded and diced
$1/_3$ cup chopped parsley

Stir in and simmer 5 minutes more.

Serves 8

VICHYSSOISE

6 leeks, sliced, white part only
½ cup butter

Wash leeks carefully under cold running water. Sauté until soft in large pot.

2 large potatoes, peeled and diced
8 cups chicken stock
1 bay leaf
1 pinch dried thyme
½ teaspoon salt
Dash of white pepper

Add to pot and simmer about 20 minutes until potatoes are tender. Remove bay leaf.

1 cup heavy cream

Add and refrigerate until cold. Purée in blender and serve chilled.

Serves 8

The better the stock, the better the soup! Serve topped with fresh chives.

BRAISED LEEKS

12 leeks, white part only

Cut each leek into four lengthwise slices. Wash carefully under cold running water and place in a kettle.

2 cups beef broth

Add and bring to a boil. Cover and reduce to a simmer. Cook for 20 to 30 minutes, until vegetables are tender.

3 tablespoons parsley
¼ teaspoon salt
Freshly ground pepper to taste

Drain and season leeks.

Serves 4

A versatile recipe. As a vegetable accompaniment, serve plain as described above, or top with a mild cheese and brown under the broiler. As a salad, chill leeks and serve with a vinaigrette dressing.

ONION SOUP

8 medium onions, chopped
4 tablespoons butter
2 tablespoons flour

Cook onions gently in butter until blond. Add flour. Cook, stirring, until golden and sizzling.

2 cups water
2 cups beef broth
1 teaspoon salt
½ teaspoon freshly ground pepper, to taste

Pour in 2 cups water. Bring to a boil and stir. Add broth and seasonings. Boil 10 minutes.

4 French rolls, or 12 slices French bread

Trim crusts, slice bread, then quarter each slice. Brown each side under broiler.

2 garlic cloves, crushed

Rub croutons with garlic.

4 cups grated Swiss cheese

Pour hot soup into 6 ovenproof bowls. Top with croutons. Cover with cheese. Broil until cheese melts.

6 tablespoons port wine

Lift crust of soup, and pour 1 tablespoon port into each bowl.

Serves 6

Terribly filling, and good! There should be no short-cuts on the croutons. Good croutons are trouble, but worth the effort. The last-minute addition of port gives this onion soup character.

SPRINGTIME CHICKEN SALAD

 6   cups chopped cooked chicken
 2   cups sliced celery
1½   cups pineapple chunks
 6   green onions, chopped finely
 2   tablespoons chopped fresh parsley

Mix and chill.

1½   cups mayonnaise
1½   cups sour cream
 ¼   cup lemon juice
 2   tablespoons grated horseradish
 1   teaspoon celery seed
 ½   teaspoon salt

Mix, chill, and toss with salad, just before serving.

Serves 12

Serve with spiced peaches and hot cheese sticks.

TOMATO ONION SALAD

4 **tomatoes, peeled and sliced**
1 **large onion, thinly sliced**
½ **cup minced fresh mint**
    Salt and freshly ground pepper
      to taste

Layer ingredients, cover and chill at least 2 hours.

Serves 4

Very refreshing in hot weather — and almost zero calories to boot!

BARBECUED HERBED ONIONS

> 4 **tablespoons soft butter**
> 1 **tablespoon minced fresh parsley**
> 1 **tablespoon minced chives**
> 1 **tablespoon minced fresh tarragon**

Mix well.

> 4 **large white onions, slashed in quarters but not quite all the way through**

Stuff equal portions of herb mixture in each onion. Wrap in foil and roast over hot coals 20 to 30 minutes.

Serves 4

Great for your bounty of onions. Substitute dried herbs if fresh ones are not available, but use only half the amount — dried herbs are more potent.

BROILED TUNA MUFFINS

      6½-ounce can tuna, drained and
         flaked
¼ cup mayonnaise
1 teaspoon prepared mustard
    Dash of Worcestershire sauce
2 tablespoons minced green peppers
¼–½ cup minced green or Bermuda onion

Mix well.

2 English muffins or hamburger buns
    Tomato slices
    Grated cheddar cheese

Split muffins or buns and spread them with mixture. Top each sandwich with tomato, then cheese. Broil until cheese melts.

Serves 2

MARINATED ONION RINGS

> 1 **cup white vinegar**
> 1 **cup water**
> $1/_3$ **cup sugar**
> 1 **cinnamon stick**
> $1/_2$ **teaspoon salt**
> $1/_2$ **teaspoon whole cloves**
> $1/_4$ **teaspoon allspice**

Simmer covered for 10 minutes.

> 1 **medium sweet onion, sliced**
> 1 **medium red onion, sliced**

Separate onions into rings. Pour hot liquid over onions. Cover and chill at least 4 hours. Drain to serve.

Serves 4

FRENCH-FRIED ONION RINGS

3 large Bermuda onions

Slice $\frac{1}{3}$ inch thick. Soak in ice water 1 hour. Separate into rings. Drain and pat dry with paper towels.

1 cup sifted flour
$\frac{1}{2}$ teaspoon baking soda
$\frac{1}{2}$ teaspoon salt
1 egg, beaten
1 cup buttermilk

Beat together until smooth.

Corn oil for deep frying

Dip onion rings in batter and deep-fry in hot oil about 5 minutes. Drain. Can be reheated in warm oven to serve.

Serves 4–6

Shamefully, many people have never tasted real French-fried onion rings. The relationship between the frozen facsimile and the real item is ludicrous. Take the time to indulge yourself in this one.

GLAZED ONIONS

6 medium onions, peeled

Cut an X in the bottom of each onion. Drop onions in a pot of boiling salted water and simmer 20 minutes or until tender. Drain and reserve ¾ cup liquid. Cut onions in half.

¼ cup butter
2 tablespoons brown sugar

Heat with reserved onion liquid in large skillet. Add onions. Cook over low heat, basting to glaze, about 15 minutes.

Serves 6

BAKED ONIONS

**3 large onions, peeled and halved
   crosswise**

Place in shallow greased baking dish.

**6 tablespoons butter
   Salt and pepper to taste
   Favorite herb to taste**

Dot butter on each onion half. Sprinkle with seasonings. Bake at 350° for about 40 minutes.

VARIATIONS

Top each onion with thick slice of tomato.

Mix grated cheddar cheese with mayonnaise and spread on each baked onion. Return to oven about 5 minutes to melt.

Serves 4–6

OVEN FONDUE

French bread, cubed
Swiss cheese, sliced
Onions, sliced
Salt and pepper
Butter

Repeat layers in a buttered casserole, ending with the bread and more butter.

Beef bouillon

Pour over all so that top layer is covered. Cook at 375° for 1 hour.

No proportions given — a do-as-you-please recipe. Whatever is in the pantry will be correct. Definitely easy.

MORE ONIONS

4 cups sliced onions
$1/4$ cup butter

Sauté until soft. Place in a casserole.

2 eggs, beaten
1 cup sour cream
Sprinkle of salt and pepper

Mix well and pour over onions.

$2/3$ cup grated Parmesan cheese

Sprinkle on top. Bake at 425° for 20 to 25 minutes.

Serves 6

An excellent side dish with roast meats or poultry.

ONION PUDDING

3 cups finely sliced onions
3 tablespoons butter

Cook over very low heat about 30 minutes. Do not let onions color.

$^2/_3$ cup grated Parmesan cheese
$^1/_4$ cup flour
2 eggs, beaten
$^2/_3$ cup milk
Salt and pepper to taste

Whisk until smooth. Stir in onions. Place in buttered gratin dish and bake 20 minutes at 400°.

Serves 4

A classic country American dish.

ONIONS IN CHEESE SAUCE

**4 large white onions, peeled and
  halved**
4 tablespoons butter

Place onions in buttered baking dish. Top with
butter. Bake uncovered 30 to 40 minutes at 350°.

2 tablespoons butter
2 tablespoons flour

Melt butter, stir in flour, and cook, stirring for
several minutes.

1 cup milk
½ cup grated cheddar cheese
2 tablespoons vermouth
  Salt and pepper to taste

Add, gradually, to butter-flour mixture, stirring
until thickened. Pour over baked onions.

**1 cup salted peanuts or sautéed
  almonds**

Sprinkle atop. Bake 10 to 15 minutes more.

Serves 8

GREEN-ONION QUICHE

2 cups chopped green onions and tops
4 tablespoons butter

Parboil onions 4 minutes. Drain. Sauté briefly in butter.

3 eggs, beaten
1 cup cream
1 cup grated Swiss cheese
Salt and pepper to taste
6 slices bacon, cooked and crumbled

Mix in a bowl. Add onions.

Quiche pastry shell (p. 465),
partially baked

Pour custard into pastry crust. Bake at 400° for 30 minutes, then at 375° until set. Let sit at least 10 minutes before cutting.

Serves 6

Minced cooked ham may be substituted for bacon.

ONION PIE

40 soda crackers
6 tablespoons melted butter

Whirl crackers in blender, half at a time. Stir in butter and press into 10-inch pie plate.

2 tablespoons butter
2 large onions, sliced thinly

Melt butter. Add onions, and sauté until golden. Spoon into pie shell.

$^1/_3$ pound cheddar cheese, grated
1 medium green chile, minced
(or 2 tablespoons canned)

Sprinkle cheese and chile atop onions.

3 eggs, beaten
$^1/_4$ teaspoon salt
$^1/_8$ teaspoon pepper
$1^1/_2$ cups milk, scalded

Mix eggs, salt and pepper. Add milk slowly, beating constantly. Pour over cheese. Bake at 350° for 25 minutes. Let stand 10 minutes before serving.

Serves 6

STUFFED ONIONS

4 large onions

Peel and parboil for 25 minutes. Cut slice from top and scoop out centers. Drain. Fill with one of the stuffings below.

Serves 4

Hamburger Stuffing

1 pound ground beef
2 small peeled and diced tomatoes
¼ teaspoon oregano or basil
Dash of Worcestershire sauce, salt, and pepper

Combine and stuff onions. Place in a square baking dish and cover with foil. Bake at 350° for 45 minutes to 1 hour.

Spinach Stuffing

1½ cups cooked spinach
4 tablespoons mayonnaise
1 tablespoon lemon juice
Salt and curry powder to taste

Combine and stuff onions. Place in a square baking dish and bake at 350° for 30 minutes.

Lemony Liver Stuffing

4 slices of bacon

Fry bacon until crisp. Crumble bacon and set aside.

½ pound liver
¼ teaspoon salt
Freshly ground pepper

Fry liver in bacon fat, 4 minutes on each side. Remove liver and season. Pour off bacon fat.

1½ tablespoons butter
1 tablespoon parsley
1 tablespoon lemon juice
The reserved bacon

Sauté in the same skillet. Scrape up crust on the bottom of the pan. Pour into a blender.

½ cup fresh bread crumbs
½ cup scooped-out onion centers

Add to blender with reserved liver and purée. Stuff onions with mixture. Place in a square baking dish and cover with foil. Bake at 350° for 30 minutes, or until center is firm.

CHICKEN AND ONIONS STASHKA

**2 fryers, quartered
Seasoned flour**

Dredge chicken with flour and arrange in large shallow baking dish.

**6 medium onions, sliced
Dashes of salt and pepper**

Cover chicken.

3–4 cups chicken broth

Use just enough to barely cover onions.

½ cup butter

Dot over onions. Bake at 350° uncovered 1 to 1½ hours, turning chicken once.

Serves 4

Chicken turns a beautiful golden brown and liquid becomes gravy. Potatoes are nice baked with this Lithuanian casserole.

SOUBISE SAUCE

2 tablespoons butter
2 tablespoons flour

Melt butter, stir in flour, and cook, stirring, for several minutes.

2 cups beef broth
¼ teaspoon salt
¼ teaspoon white pepper

Add. Cook and stir until thickened.

4 onions, minced
4 tablespoons butter

Cook over low heat about 20 minutes. Do not let onions color. Add to thickened sauce and simmer 15 minutes to blend.

3–4 tablespoons light cream
1–2 tablespoons softened butter

Blend in before serving.

2½ cups

This is the classic French onion sauce. Marvelous on almost any kind of meat. For an elegant menu, top artichoke bottoms with broiled boned lamb chops and cover with soubise.

FRENCH ONION LOAF

    1   **large onion, finely minced**
    ¼   **cup butter**
    3   **tablespoons grated Parmesan cheese**
    1   **tablespoon minced fresh parsley**
    1   **tablespoon sesame seeds**
    1   **clove garlic, finely minced**

Heat together until butter melts. Set aside to cool.

    2   **cups flour**
  1½   **teaspoons salt**
    ½   **cup hot (not boiling) water**
    ¼   **cup butter**
    1   **egg**
    1   **package dry yeast dissolved in**
          ¼ cup warm water

Combine in large mixing bowl. Beat 2 minutes at medium speed.

    2   **cups flour**

Stir in. Cover and let rise 1 hour. Punch down and knead a few minutes on floured surface until no longer sticky. Roll out to 18 by 12 inches. Spread with onion filling. Cut lengthwise into 3 4-inch strips. Fold each strip over lengthwise to make 2-inch strip. Braid on a buttered cookie sheet. Cover and let rise 1 hour. Bake 30 minutes at 350°.

1 loaf

PEAS

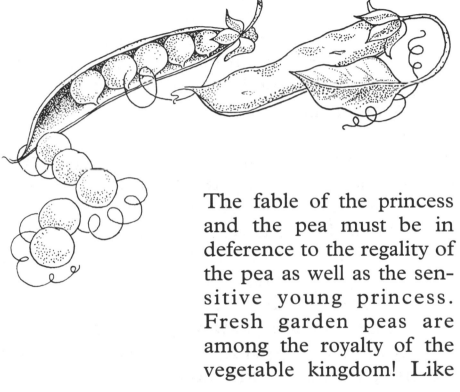

The fable of the princess and the pea must be in deference to the regality of the pea as well as the sensitive young princess. Fresh garden peas are among the royalty of the vegetable kingdom! Like corn, they must be cooked and eaten immediately. They have little in common with the days-old peas one finds at the local market. Fresh peas squeak and sing when rubbed. They are sweet and refined, and have a lightly crunchy texture. It is only fitting that these bright, grass-green delicacies signal the arrival of spring and the beginning of many months of vegetable harvest.

Sugar peas, also known as snow peas, are cultivated for the edible pod, which is very crunchy and moist. Sugar peas are a prominent vegetable in Chinese cuisine and through that medium have been widely introduced in the United States. They have the same growing requirements as their fully developed pea cousins, but they are picked before the pods bulge.

Peas are considered one of the energy vegetables, as they are high in protein, 6 to 7 percent. They are packed with vitamins, including the rarer Vitamin E.

The Growing Peas are rather particular about the weather, preferring temperatures averaging around 75° and thriving in a cool-weather climate. Plant the seeds very early, before anything else, at the end of the subfreezing weather. The ground may be still hard, so it is advantageous to prepare the bed in the fall, or grow them all winter in frost-free climates. Always plant peas by seed, as they do not transplant. The seeds come in two varieties, wrinkled and smooth. Wrinkled seeds are a late development (smooth-seeded peas may be as old as two thousand years) cultivated for their sweetness. Most gardeners prefer the wrinkled seeds for this reason, even though they should be planted a week or two later than smooth peas. Plant the seeds 1½ inches deep at 1½ inch intervals. Space rows 2 feet apart. Drop 2 seeds at each spot and later thin to stronger plant.

Peas are historically a vine plant, although a

bush variety has been developed. As with snap beans, the vine variety outproduces the bush plant. The vine grows 3 to 6 feet high, and the bush reaches 1½ feet. Depending on variety, peas are ready to harvest 55 to 80 days after planting.

The Harvest A pea is ready for harvest when the pod is bulging with peas, but is still bright green. Do not let peas begin to lose color and mature. At maturity a chemical change takes place which causes the sugar content to decrease rapidly, as the pea is drying to seed. Peas may be difficult to pull from the plant, so hold the vine firmly with one hand and pull the pod with the other.

The Basics
1 pound peas in pods = 1–2 cups shelled peas = 3–4 servings.
$^2/_3$ cup cooked peas (3.5 ounces) = 71 calories, 12.1 grams carbohydrates, 5.4 grams protein, some vitamins A, E, C.
10-foot row = 7 pounds.

The Storage Peas deteriorate and toughen after harvest. They lose sugar, vitamins, and texture, so it is best not to store them at all. But, if necessary, store them unshelled in a plastic bag in the refrigerator. They are usable but have lost their spectacularly good qualities after 24 hours.

Freezing Shell and scald for 1 minute. Chill in cold water. Drain. Package in convenient-size bags, label, and freeze.

The Cooking Peas are delicious either hot or cold, but require sufficient cooking for all preparations.

Basic Preparation Bring 1 inch water to boil. Add 3 pea pods, then peas, and a dash of sugar. Cover with 3 lettuce leaves and 3 more pea pods. Cook uncovered about 5 minutes. Remove pods and leaves. Drain and add salt, pepper, and butter.

Complementary Herbs Basil, marjoram, mint, and nutmeg.

SPRINGTIME MINT SOUP

6 cups unshelled peas

Rinse, shell, and put pods and peas in large pot.

4 cups chicken stock
1 large onion, chopped
1 teaspoon sugar
3 mint sprigs

Add to pot and bring to a boil. Then simmer uncovered 20 to 30 minutes. Purée all in blender and then strain through a sieve.

3 tablespoons butter
2 tablespoons flour
1 cup light cream or milk

Melt butter, stir in flour, and cook, stirring, for several minutes. Blend in cream and stir to thicken. Add to pot along with pea purée.

Salt and pepper to taste
Fresh mint sprigs

Season soup and garnish with mint.

Serves 6

CURRIED GREEN PEA SOUP

  2   **tablespoons butter**
  1   **tablespoon oil**
  1   **onion, minced**
  1   **clove garlic, minced**

Sauté 5 minutes in saucepan.

  1   **cup peas**
  ¼   **teaspoon salt**
2–3   **teaspoons curry powder**

Add to pan and simmer until peas are soft. Remove from heat.

  2   **tablespoons flour**
  2   **cups chicken broth**

Stir in flour, then broth. Reheat to a boil, then purée in blender or rub through a sieve. (Freeze, if desired, at this point.)

  ¾   **cup light cream**

Add. Chill to serve cold or reheat.

Serves 4

Diced chicken meat may be added for a main-dish soup. Garnish with chopped chives or minced green onions.

RICE AND PEA SOUP

¼ cup butter
¼ cup minced onion

Sauté until golden.

1½ cups peas
½ teaspoon salt

Add and continue cooking about 4 minutes.

5 cups chicken broth
¾ cup raw rice
Juice of 1–2 lemons
Pepper to taste

Bring broth to a boil, add rice, cover, and simmer about 20 minutes. Combine with pea mixture and season with more salt, pepper, and lemon.

Minced fresh parsley

Ladle soup into bowls and sprinkle with parsley.

Serves 6

SHRIMP RISOTTO SALAD

1   cup peas, cooked
2½ cups cold, cooked rice
1   cup diced celery
2   green onions, minced
2   tomatoes, quartered
½–1 pound fresh, cooked shrimp
6   ounces marinated artichoke hearts

Combine in large bowl.

Oil from artichoke hearts
2   **tablespoons white wine vinegar**
1   **teaspoon anchovy paste**
1   **teaspoon sharp prepared mustard**
½   **teaspoon ground dried sage**

Mix. Pour over salad and toss gently. Chill at least 1 hour.

2   **hard-boiled eggs, quartered**
Minced fresh parsley

Decorate salad before serving.

Serves 6

A perfect summer luncheon dish with croissants and chilled wine.

MINTED PEAS

2 tablespoons butter
½ cup chopped green onions

Sauté 3 minutes.

2 cups peas
3 tablespoons water
2 tablespoons chopped fresh mint
1 teaspoon sugar
1 teaspoon lemon juice

Add. Cover and simmer 5 to 8 minutes, until peas are tender.

Serves 4

PETITS POIS
À LA FRANÇAISE

3 **cups peas**
1 **medium head Boston lettuce,
shredded**
½ **teaspoon salt**
1–2 **tablespoons sugar**
4 **tablespoons minced scallions**
4 **tablespoons butter**

Place in saucepan and lightly squeeze together with hands to bruise peas. Barely cover with cold water. Cover and cook on medium-high heat 10 to 15 minutes until peas are tender and liquid has evaporated.

Serves 4–6

Translated: little peas, French style. Use only little peas for this. If they are fresh from the vine, use the lesser amount of sugar. A beautiful preparation.

CHINESE FRIED RICE AND PEAS

    4 **tablespoons oil**
   ¼ cup minced onions
   ¼ cup sliced mushrooms

Stir-fry over moderate heat.

    2 **cups cooked rice**
    3 **tablespoons chicken broth**
    1 **tablespoon soy sauce**
    1 **tablespoon butter**
    1 **teaspoon salt**

Add and stir until rice is very hot.

    1 **cup green peas, parboiled and
       drained**
    4 **eggs, well beaten**

Add and stir over heat until eggs cook.

Serves 3–4

Leftover meat, seafood, or poultry can be added to make this an inexpensive main dish.

STIR-FRIED SNOW PEAS

  2 **tablespoons peanut oil**
 ¼ **cup sliced green onions**
  2 **cups snow peas**

Sauté quickly over high heat just until vegetables are coated with oil.

  1 **teaspoon sugar**
  1 **teaspoon minced fresh ginger (optional)**
  6 **tablespoons chicken broth**

Add, cover and cook 3 minutes over medium heat.

  2 **tablespoons chicken broth**
  2 **tablespoons cornstarch**
  1 **teaspoon soy sauce**
  1 **can water chestnuts, drained and chopped (optional)**

Mix together and stir quickly into peas, cooking until sauce thickens.

Serves 4

RISI E BISI

¼ **cup butter**
1 **onion, chopped**
1 **slice bacon, diced**
1 **stalk celery, chopped**

Sauté in large skillet until onion is soft and bacon done.

½ **cup diced ham**
¾ **cup uncooked rice**

Add and sauté 5 minutes.

1¾ **cups chicken broth**
½ **teaspoon salt**
¼ **teaspoon pepper**

Add. Bring to a boil. Cover. Reduce heat to simmer. Cook 20 minutes.

2 **cups peas**

Stir in peas. Cook covered 10 minutes more. Rice should be moist.

Grated Parmesan cheese

Serve with lots of freshly grated Parmesan cheese.

Serves 4

Rice and peas, in the Venetian manner.

FETTUCINI ALLA BISI

    2 **tablespoons butter**
    2 **cups sliced mushrooms**
    2 **cups slivered cooked ham**
    ½ **cup minced onion**

Sauté 5 minutes.

    1 **cup peas, parboiled 5 minutes and**
        drained

Add and keep warm over very low heat.

    ½ **cup heavy cream**
    6 **tablespoons butter**

Bring to a boil in a large pan and cook until shiny
bubbles form.

    3 **cups hot cooked fettucini or**
        egg noodles

Add to pan along with pea mixture.

    1 **cup grated Parmesan cheese**
    ¾ **cup heavy cream, at room**
        temperature

Toss in and serve immediately.

Serves 4

*In Italy, fettucini is customarily served as a first course.
Unfortunately, it requires last-minute preparation. By
using a chafing dish, you can create a dramatic beginning to your dinner party.*

ARROZ CON POLLO

> 2 **cloves garlic, minced**
> 1 **tablespoon dried oregano**
> **Juice of ½ lemon**
> 8 **pieces of chicken**

Rub garlic, oregano, and lemon juice into chicken. Let stand 1 hour.

> ½ **cup olive oil**

Sauté chicken until brown. Remove.

> 1 **onion, chopped**
> 1 **green pepper, diced**

Sauté in same oil until soft.

> 1 **cup uncooked rice**
> 1½ **cups chicken broth**
> 3½ **cups fresh or canned stewed**
>   **tomatoes with their juice**
> 1 **bay leaf**
> ½ **teaspoon dried oregano**

Add. Bring to boil. Stir to break up tomatoes, simmer over low heat about 15 minutes.

> 3 **cups peas**

Stir in peas and cook covered 7 minutes. Liquid should be absorbed.

> 3 **pimentos, cut in pieces**

Decorate top with pimento.

Serves 6–8

Arroz con pollo means rice with chicken. This classic Spanish dish is always served with peas, and frequently asparagus and artichoke hearts as well.

PEPPERS

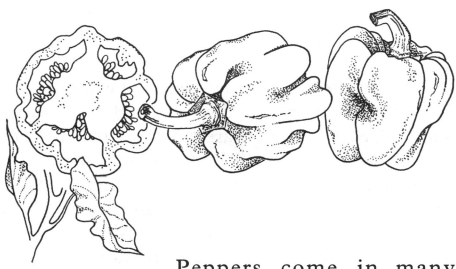

Peppers come in many shapes, sizes, colors, and flavors. However, the black peppercorn from which we derive our table pepper is not included in this vast range. Peppers, whether sweet green or the hottest chili, grow on shrubs about 2 feet by 2 feet which are perennials in their native warm-weather climate in South America. Most North Americans are familiar with the sweet green pepper, but Americans from Mexico to Peru enjoy an array of hot, colorful peppers in their native dishes. Even the sweet green pepper will display glorious summer color if left to mature on the vine. It will turn red or yellow, and the flavor will sweeten. Some chili peppers can be quite palatable to the novice, while others are too hot for a steel stomach. The hotness in peppers is attributed to an oil called capsicum. Some varieties (from least hot to most hot) include the pimento; the California long green, which is essential for chili rellenos; the jalapeño, a favorite in Mexican cuisine; and the tiny red chili used in Tabasco sauce.

The Growing Peppers are heat and water lovers. They require warm, hot days and nights no colder than 55°. Some peppers are more particular about their climate. The small fruits can withstand hotter days, which is logical since they are the "hottest." Sometimes the blossoms and fruits fall to the ground in low humidity or excessive heat. The pepper seed is very slow germinating. Do not plant directly in the ground. Transplanted seedlings require about 30 days. Set plants at 1½ foot intervals in rows spaced 2½ feet apart.

The Harvest Sweet green peppers are picked while still crisp, no more than 4 inches by 3 inches. Cut peppers with scissors to avoid damage to the branch. Be sure to leave some peppers on the plant until they are red! The green pepper is as high in vitamin C as tomatoes and as high in vitamin B as most greens.

The Basics
1 pound = 2 medium green sweet peppers = 1 cup chopped.

1 raw green sweet pepper (3.5 ounces) = 22 calories, 4.8 grams carbohydrates, 1.2 grams protein, four times daily recommended vitamin C, half recommended daily vitamin A.
6 plants (4 sweet green and 2 hot) = about 150 peppers.

The Storage Refrigerate unwashed in plastic sacks for one week in the crisper drawer. Peppers, especially hot ones, can also be dried.

Freezing Sweet peppers may be frozen without blanching, although they lose crispness. Simply chop, package, and freeze.

The Cooking The veins and seeds of sweet peppers should be removed. (Remember, when using hot peppers, that the seeds and veins are the hottest part.) Some recipes call for peeling the skin of a pepper. They need not be peeled until they are very mature. And it is not always necessary if they are very fresh. To peel off the waxy coating, burn the peppers on top of a gas or electric range. Immediately place in a plastic bag for 15 to 20 minutes, then peel and lightly rinse clean. If peppers are to be stuffed, parboil them for 6 to 8 minutes.

Complementary Herbs Basil, cumin, garlic, oregano.

FRESH ENCHILADA SAUCE

2 medium onions, chopped
2 cloves garlic, minced
1 sweet green pepper, chopped
1 carrot, finely chopped
1 celery stalk, finely chopped
4 tablespoons oil

Sauté until soft.

1 cup tomato sauce
9 jalapeño peppers, seeded and
     minced
2 teaspoons sugar
1 teaspoon salt
$^1/_4$ teaspoon ground cumin
$^1/_8$ teaspoon dried oregano
1 fresh basil leaf, chopped

Add and simmer 10 minutes.

1 pint

*Three California long green peppers may be substi-
tuted for the 2 jalapeño peppers.*

HOT PEPPER TACO SAUCE

- 10 fresh jalapeño peppers, seeded and deveined
- 9 medium onions
- 4 tomatoes, peeled

Chop finely.

- 1 cup white vinegar
- ½ cup sugar
- ½ teaspoon salt

Combine and add to above. Simmer until thick.

1 quart

Hot, hot, hot! To make chili salsa, halve the amount of peppers.

CHILI-COTTAGE CHEESE DIP

   1 **pint small-curd cottage cheese**
 2–4 **long green chili peppers,**
       peeled and chopped
   2 **tomatoes, peeled and diced**
   3 **green onions, including tops,**
       chopped
   1 **teaspoon salt**
   ½ **teaspoon Worcestershire sauce**

Mix. Chill for 3 hours.

3 cups

Serve as an hors d'oeuvre with tortilla chips or with crackers for a low-calorie lunch.

PICKLED PEPPERS

3 cups sugar
3 cups cider vinegar
1 teaspoon mustard seed
1 teaspoon celery seed
1 clove garlic, minced
1 teaspoon turmeric
$^1/_3$ cup salt

Bring to a boil.

8–10 cups sweet green pepper
strips or chunks
2 cups sliced onions

Pour hot liquid over. Cool, cover and refrigerate overnight at least. Keeps 1 to 2 weeks.

9 pints

Next time Peter Piper picks a peck of peppers, try.

STIR-FRIED BEEF AND GREEN PEPPERS

> 3 tablespoons peanut oil
> 1 clove garlic, mashed

Heat together in large skillet. Remove garlic.

> 1 yellow onion, sliced
> 1 large sweet green pepper, sliced

Over high heat add to skillet and stir quickly for about 3 minutes. Remove.

> ½ pound flank or round steak,
>   cut in thin slices across the grain
> 1 teaspoon grated fresh ginger

Add to skillet with more oil if necessary. Stir until pink is gone.

> ½ cup beef broth
> 2 teaspoons cornstarch
> 2 tablespoons soy sauce

Combine and add to skillet along with green peppers and onions. Stir about 2 minutes to thicken.

Serves 2–3

Serve with a bowl of steaming rice and crisp marinated cucumbers. One or two chopped tomatoes may be added during the final stages of cooking.

PEPERONATA

1 celery stalk
2 small zucchini

Cut into thick slices.

½ small eggplant

Do not peel. Cut into chunks.

6 medium tomatoes

Peel and quarter.

1 large white onion, chopped
1 clove garlic, minced
3–4 fresh basil leaves, chopped
1 beef bouillon cube, dissolved in
 ¼ cup hot water
Salt and pepper to taste

Add to cut-up vegetables and mix together in a heavy kettle.

4 tablespoons olive oil

Drizzle olive oil over top. Cover and simmer 30 minutes, stirring occasionally.

4 large sweet green peppers
4 large sweet red peppers

Remove seeds and pith from peppers and cut into thick slices. Stir peppers into pot. Simmer covered for 30 minutes more.

Serves 6

CHILI RELLENOS

2 onions, finely minced and sautéed in oil
¼ cup water
4 cups tomato sauce

Combine and simmer for 30 minutes.

¾ pound Monterey Jack cheese, cut in finger slices
10–12 long green chili peppers, peeled, seeded, deveined, slit lengthwise
Flour

Stuff cheese into peppers. Pat in flour to coat.

4 eggs, separated

Beat egg whites until stiff. Beat yolks lightly and fold into whites. Coat peppers with mixture.

½ cup oil

Fry peppers in hot oil, about 3 minutes per side. Drain on brown paper bags, then place in oven-proof dish. Pour sauce over and reheat if necessary.

Serves 4–6

This Mexican recipe is so authentic that the donor doesn't even speak English.

SAUTÉED RED AND GREEN PEPPERS

    2 **large sweet green peppers, sliced**
    2 **large sweet red peppers, sliced**
    ¼ **cup olive oil**
    2 **cloves garlic, minced**
       Salt and pepper to taste

Sauté all about 5 minutes. Do not overcook, as it gets mushy.

Serves 4

You can use only red or green, but both together are prettiest. This Italian treatment of peppers is nice with veal. Serve hot as a vegetable dish or chill and serve as a salad.

MEXICAN BEEF STEW

3½ **pounds stew meat, cubed**
3 **tablespoons oil**

Brown. Remove meat.

2 **tablespoons oil**
2 **cups chopped onions**
4 **cloves garlic, mashed**

Sauté in large pot.

8 **tablespoons chopped jalapeño peppers, seeded and deveined**
1 ½ **teaspoons ground cumin**
2 **cups beef broth**
2–3 **cups chopped tomatoes**
6 **ounces tomato paste**
1 **tablespoon salt**
1 **teaspoon sugar**

Add to pot. Add meat. Simmer 2 hours or until meat is tender.

1–3 **tablespoons cornmeal**

Stir in until sauce is thickened.

Serves 6

Serve with rice, refried beans, flour tortillas and butter, and zucchini in salsa verde (page 351).

TORTILLA-CHILI CASSEROLE

1 **medium onion, chopped**
2 **tablespoons oil**

Sauté until tender.

4 **jalapeño peppers, peeled and chopped**
1 **cup cream**
1 **cup tomato purée**
½ **teaspoon salt**

Add and simmer 10 minutes.

½ **pound Monterey Jack cheese, grated**
1 **dozen corn tortillas, cut in strips**
2 **tablespoons butter**

In a greased casserole dish, layer half the tortillas, half the sauce and half the cheese. Repeat. Dot with butter. Bake at 350° for 30 minutes.

Serves 6

A perfect, simple side dish for barbecued hamburgers and corn on the cob.

CHILI QUICHE

1½   cups shredded Monterey Jack cheese
½   cup shredded cheddar cheese
    Quiche pastry shell (p. 465),
       partially baked

Sprinkle cheese in crust.

2   green chili peppers, peeled, seeded,
       diced
1   cup light cream
3   eggs

Beat together. Pour over cheese.

½   cup grated cheddar cheese

Sprinkle atop. Bake at 325° for 30 to 40 minutes.
Let stand 15 minutes before serving.

Serves 6

*Diced ham or cooked bacon bits make a tasty addition
to this light luncheon dish.*

STUFFED GREEN PEPPERS

6 large green peppers

Cut off stem tops and hollow out seeds and membranes; discard. Parboil peppers for 5 minutes and drain. Place in an oiled baking dish and stuff.

Serves 4–6

Stuffed peppers freeze well when placed in individual plastic bags. Keep a supply on hand for last-minute dinners.

Ham Stuffing

2 tablespoons butter
3 cups cooked ham, minced
1 large onion, chopped
1 clove garlic, minced
3 large tomatoes, chopped

Sauté in a large skillet for 20 minutes.

3 slices toasted bread, well crumbled
Salt and pepper
Light cream

Add crumbs and seasonings to skillet. If necessary, add cream to moisten. Stuff peppers and bake at 350° for 30 minutes.

Quiche Filling

8 slices cooked bacon, minced
1 cup grated cheddar cheese
1 cup grated Swiss cheese
1 cup light cream
3 eggs

Combine and mix well. Spoon into the peppers. Bake at 350° for 45 to 60 minutes, until the centers are firm.

Seafood Stuffing

4 tablespoons butter
1 large onion, chopped
½ cup diced celery

Sauté in a large skillet for 5 minutes.

½ pound large cooked shrimp,
**   peeled and chopped**
1 tablespoon flour
3 tablespoons tomato sauce
**   Dash of Tabasco**
**   Salt and pepper**

Add to vegetables and stir well. Simmer for 10 minutes.

2 cups cooked rice
1 six-ounce can crabmeat or lobster
**   Bread crumbs**

Stir in rice and crabmeat and stuff peppers. Top with breadcrumbs. Bake at 350° for 30 minutes.

Corned Beef Hash Stuffing

1 sixteen-ounce can of corned beef hash
1 cup grated mild cheese
4 green onions, minced
¼ cup ketchup
1 teaspoon oregano

Combine well and stuff peppers.

Grated Parmesan cheese

Sprinkle cheese on peppers and bake at 350° for 35 to 45 minutes.

Sausage or Beef Stuffing

4 tablespoons butter
½ cup minced green onions
¼ pound mushrooms, diced
1 clove garlic, minced

Sauté in a large skillet for 10 minutes.

1 tablespoon oil
½ pound pork sausage or lean ground beef

Brown meat in a separate skillet, draining off grease. Add meat to the vegetables.

2 cups cooked rice
2 beaten eggs
Salt and pepper

¼ cup grated Parmesan cheese

Add, combine well, and stuff the peppers. Bake at 350° for 30 minutes.

QUICK-AND-EASY STUFFED PEPPERS

½ pound ground chuck
1 small onion, minced
5 crushed crackers (or ½ cup)
¾ teaspoon salt
¼ teaspoon pepper
¼ cup uncooked rice
¼ cup water

Mix together well.

2–3 sweet green peppers

Cut in halves lengthwise, remove seeds and cores, fill with meat mixture, and place in buttered casserole.

1½ cups tomato sauce
1 small clove garlic, minced

Mix and pour over peppers. Bake at 350° for 1 hour. Uncover and bake 15 more minutes.

Serves 4

Extremely simple! There is no cooking of rice or blanching of peppers. Throw two or three meals' worth together at once and freeze the others in family portions.

HOMINY AND CALIFORNIA LONG GREEN CHILI PEPPERS

2 tablespoons grated onion
$^1/_2$ cup sour cream
$^2/_3$ cup coarsely shredded
    Monterey Jack cheese
3 California long green chilis,
    toasted, peeled, seeded and
    chopped (or canned)
    Salt and pepper to taste
    1-pound can white hominy, drained

Mix well, and put in buttered casserole.

3 tablespoons bread crumbs
1 tablespoon butter

Sprinkle casserole with crumbs and dot with butter. Bake at 350° for 30 minutes.

Serves 4

Add ground beef for an easy Texan dinner.

POTATOES

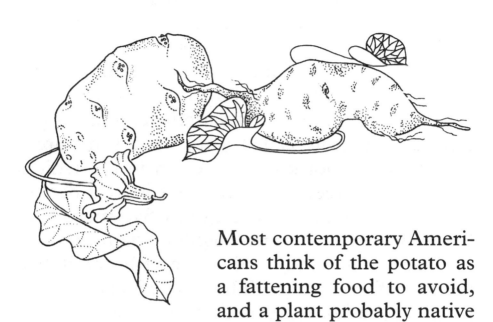

Most contemporary Americans think of the potato as a fattening food to avoid, and a plant probably native to the British Isles. Wrong on both counts! Yes, compared to most vegetables, the potato is high in calories and carbohydrates, but it contains more protein and is a good source of iron, niacin, phosphorus, potassium, calcium, and vitamins C and B. It is satisfying and offers much for its weight in calories. It's usually what you put on it that's so fattening. As to the Europeans and potatoes, they did not begin cultivating the potato until the sixteenth or seventeenth century. The potato is native to Chile, brought north by the Indians. It was finally a major crop in

Ireland by the mid-seventeenth century.

There are three major varieties of *Solanum tuberosum:* the baking potato, Idaho or Maine, which is dry and mealy; the large boiling called long white potato; and the small New Red. All require 80 to 100 days for full maturation.

The sweet potato, *Ipomoea batatas,* is not related to the white potato. It is a tuber plant of the morning glory family. There are forty varieties, one of which has yellow-orange flesh and is the sweetest and moistest variety. This sweet potato is mistakenly called yam. True yams are a tropical plant not grown or eaten in the United States. The sweet potato requires a great deal of room for vining, and it requires five months of hot weather (and warm nights). Plant sprouts, not tubers, in sandy soil. Cure well about two weeks before storage. The cooked and puréed pulp may be frozen. As with winter squash, freshness is not a nutrition factor.

The Growing Be sure to obtain certified seed potatoes. Market potatoes might carry disease or be treated to delay sprouting. Cut the potato in four or five pieces with at least two eyes in each piece. Dry one or two days. Plant with eyes up and cover with 4 to 5 inches of soil. Hill up the soil 2 inches around the plant when the foliage is about 5 inches. Potatoes thrive in cool weather, around 60°. Supply steady moisture. Drought causes knobby potatoes. Although potatoes generally require considerable space, they can be successfully grown in containers if rich, loose, well-drained soil is provided.

The Harvest Dig out small new potatoes any time after the plant flowers, but be careful not to disturb the smaller tubers. Young potatoes, 1 to 2 inches, are so good they may be eaten raw like an apple. Harvest mature potatoes when the foliage starts to die down.

The Basics
1 pound = 3 four-inch white potatoes = 2 cups sliced.
1 four-inch cooked white potato (3.5 ounces) = 76 calories, 17.1 grams carbohydrates, 2.1 grams protein.
10-foot row = 40–50 pounds potatoes.

The Storage Store potatoes in a cool, moist, dark place. Wrapping is not required. Too much sunlight on white potatoes may cause green spots, caused by solanine, which are mildly poisonous. (The tomatolike fruit on the plant top and the sprouts are poisonous as well.) Potatoes may be stored for 2 to 3 months.

Freezing Raw potatoes should not be frozen, but many cooked potato dishes freeze quite nicely. Twice-baked potatoes (page 317) are great, since they can be wrapped in foil to freeze and put right into the oven from the freezer. Be sure to cook all potato dishes while still frozen — as they will get mealy if thawed first.

The Cooking Potatoes may be cooked whole or cut in any fashion. They may be boiled, baked, fried, or roasted. In any event, wash thoroughly and pick off sprouts. Cut out the eyes, which may contain solanine.

Basic Preparation *Baked potatoes:* Use the large Idaho or smaller Maine baking potato. Bake 45 minutes at 375°. After 20 minutes prick with a fork to allow air to escape. *Boiled potatoes:* Boil small potatoes, or large potatoes cut up, 15 minutes covered in salted water. Drain. Serve with butter or mash with milk or cream and butter.

Complementary Herbs Basil, dill, nutmeg, parsley.

CREAM OF POTATO SOUP

4 **cups peeled and diced potatoes**
1½ **cups chicken stock**
1 **sliced medium onion**

Combine and simmer 30 minutes. Purée in blender.

2 **cups light cream**
½ **cup white wine**
   Salt and pepper to taste

Stir into purée and heat gently.

¼ **cup minced fresh parsley**

Sprinkle with parsley and serve.

Serves 6–8

NEW POTATO SALAD

8 large new potatoes, cooked, peeled,
   and cut into 1-inch cubes
½ cup chopped green onion
½ cup chopped fresh parsley

Combine in salad bowl.

1 cup olive oil
¼ cup tarragon vinegar
1 tablespoon Worcestershire sauce
1 tablespoon sugar
1 teaspoon salt
½ teaspoon dry mustard
2 cloves garlic, minced

Mix and pour over salad while potatoes are warm.
Toss gently. Let stand at least 4 hours at room
temperature, stirring occasionally.

Serves 8

POTATO AND APPLE SALAD

¼ cup heavy cream
2 tablespoons white wine vinegar
2 teaspoons grated onion
1 teaspoon salt
Dash of pepper
½ cup olive oil

Mix well in blender or jar.

2 pounds new potatoes
¼ cup dry white wine
1 pound McIntosh apples,
    peeled and thinly sliced

Cook potatoes 15 to 20 minutes in salted water, until tender. Drain, peel, slice ¼ inch thick, and toss with wine. Add dressing to apples and potatoes.

Serves 4–6

Delightful — not as heavy as most potato salads.

HOT GERMAN POTATO SALAD

**6 medium potatoes, cooked,
    peeled, thinly sliced**

Arrange in overlapping rows in a shallow casserole.

6 slices bacon

Fry, drain, and dice, leaving fat in pan.

1 small yellow onion, chopped

Fry onion in bacon fat until tender.

2 tablespoons flour
3 tablespoons sugar
1 teaspoon salt
    Freshly ground pepper to taste

Mix and stir into onions.

Scant ½ cup vinegar
¾ cup water

Add to onion mixture and stir about 2 minutes until thickened. Pour over potatoes.

Minced green onions

Garnish with bacon and minced onions. Serve warm.

Serves 4–6

An excellent sweet-sour salad or vegetable entrée.

310

OLD-FASHIONED POTATO SALAD

>   8 baking potatoes, sliced
>   1 inch thick
> 1 ½ cups chicken stock

Combine and bring to boil. Then simmer covered until just tender. Drain.

> ½–1 cup French dressing (see page 226)

Pour over hot potatoes to cover and absorb. Let cool. Dice potatoes. (They will be firm and not mushy when sliced after dressing has been added.)

>   ½ Bermuda onion, chopped
>   2 sweet pickles, minced
>   1 tablespoon sweet pickle juice
>   ½ cup minced celery
>   2 hard-cooked eggs, sliced
>   Mayonnaise to moisten
>   Salt and pepper to taste

Toss in lightly. Chill to blend flavors.

Serves 6–8

POTATO PANCAKES

6 medium potatoes, peeled
1 medium onion

Grate just before you plan to make pancakes.

1 tablespoon flour
1 teaspoon salt
3 eggs, beaten
Dash of pepper

Stir into potatoes and onions.

2–4 tablespoons bacon grease,
      oil or butter

Drop spoonfuls of batter into hot fat. Brown on one side, turn, brown on the other. Add more fat as needed. May be kept warm in a 300° oven.

Serves 4

Good with applesauce. These pancakes freeze well; just reheat while still frozen.

POTATO PUFFS

½ **cup water**
1 **tablespoon butter**

Bring to a boil.

½ **cup flour**

Add and stir until sides of pan are clean. Remove from heat.

1 **cup mashed potatoes**
2 **eggs, beaten**
¼ **teaspoon nutmeg (optional)**

Add, stirring.

Oil for deep frying

Drop mixture by teaspoonfuls into hot oil and fry 3 to 5 minutes. Drain on paper towels and serve.

Serves 4–6

COSHE

5–6 **baking potatoes, peeled and grated**
  4 **eggs, beaten**
  1 **medium onion, grated**
$^1/_4$ **teaspoon salt**
   Dash of pepper

Mix. (Combination will be runny).

   Vegetable oil

Use enough oil to cover pan $^1/_8$ inch. Carefully pour in potatoes. Bake at 350° for $1^1/_2$ hours, until brown and crusty.

  2 **cups cottage cheese**
  1 **cup sour cream**
3–5 **green onions, finely minced**
   Salt and pepper to taste

Mix all and let chill. Serve with potatoes.

Serves 4

A Lithuanian peasant recipe — a huge potato pancake served with a chilled cream topping called Vaishki.

314

DRUNKEN POTATOES

3 medium baking potatoes

Peel and slice ¼ inch thick. Arrange in a buttered 9- to 10-inch pie plate, overlapping the slices.

¼ cup vermouth
2 tablespoons butter, cut up
Generous dashes of salt and pepper

Pour vermouth over potatoes and dot with butter and seasonings. Bake at 350° to 375° about 30 minutes.

Serves 4

Terrific for a dinner party. Do the whole thing in advance and put in the onion at the last minute.

ROADSIDE POTATOES

  1   **cup milk**
1½ **teaspoons flour**
  1   **tablespoon salt**
     Dash of Tabasco
  1   **large onion, diced**

Mix well in blender to purée onion.

  4   **medium potatoes, peeled**
¼ **pound cheddar cheese**

Grate into the milk mixture. Bake in 8-inch greased pan at 350° for 1 hour 15 minutes, until golden.

Serves 6

No repertoire of potato recipes would be complete without this.

TWICE-BAKED POTATOES

7 baking potatoes

Bake at 350° for 1 to 1½ hours. Slit lengthwise, and remove pulp. Reserve the 12 best bottom skins.

2 tablespoons butter
³/₄ cup milk
¹/₃ cup sour cream
2 tablespoons minced chives
¹/₄–¹/₂ teaspoon salt
Freshly ground pepper to taste

Beat along with potato pulp with electric mixer until creamy. Spoon into shells.

Finely grated cheddar cheese
Minced chives

Top with cheese and more chives. To serve, heat at 350° for 15 minutes (30 minutes if frozen).

Serves 8–10

These can be made earlier or frozen, then reheated. Filling uses 12 of the 14 shells. All big eaters will want two helpings, so be forewarned.

CRAB-STUFFED POTATOES

4 medium potatoes, baked

Halve, scoop out pulp. Reserve shells.

4 tablespoons butter
½ cup light cream
1 tablespoon grated onion
1 teaspoon salt
1 cup grated cheddar cheese
6-ounce can crabmeat, drained

Blend well with potato pulp in order given. Fill shells.

Paprika

Sprinkle with paprika and bake at 375° to 400° about 15 minutes.

Serves 8

POTATO PUFF CASSEROLE

  4 **cups mashed potatoes**
  3 **cups cottage cheese, blended or**
    sieved
 $^3/_4$ **cup sour cream**
 $1^1/_2$ **tablespoons grated onion**
 $2^1/_2$ **teaspoons salt**
 $^1/_8$ **teaspoon pepper**
  4 **tablespoons butter**

Mix and pour into greased 2-quart casserole. Bake at 350° for 30 minutes.

 $^1/_2$ **cup slivered almonds**

Garnish with almonds, then place under broiler for a few minutes to brown.

Serves 6

High in protein!

EGGY POTATOEY

3–4 large potatoes, peeled, boiled,
     and drained
  2 tablespoons butter
     About ¼ cup milk
     Salt and pepper to taste

Mash together. Heap in a buttered casserole.

  4 eggs

Make deep holes in the surface of potatoes. Break
eggs into holes.

     Salt and pepper
     Ham, minced
     Green onion, minced (optional)
     Cheese, grated (optional)

Sprinkle in order given on top of casserole. Bake
at 350° about 25 minutes.

Serves 4

*An early California Gold Rush recipe. Fine entrée for
a family — full of nutrition, satisfying, and inexpensive.*

FANCY OVEN-BAKED POTATOES

**5–6 small boiling potatoes, peeled and
     sliced 1 inch thick**
½ cup butter
½ teaspoon salt

Trim potatoes into ovals by beveling corners if
you like. Arrange in buttered gratin dish large
enough to hold single layer. Pour in water ½ to
1 inch deep. Dot with butter and sprinkle with
salt. Cook in 425° oven for 45 minutes. Pour off
any excess water. Brown under broiler until potatoes are golden and crusty.

Serves 3–4

DANISH SCALLOPED POTATOES

   3 **cups heavy cream**
   8 **medium potatoes, peeled and sliced**
      $1/_8$ inch thick

In a saucepan pour cream to cover potatoes. Simmer over low heat for 30 minutes. Drain and reserve cream. Arrange potatoes in large shallow buttered casserole.

   $1/_2$ **teaspoon salt**
   $1/_4$ **teaspoon white pepper**

Stir seasonings into cream. Pour over potatoes.

   8 **ounces cheddar cheese, grated**
   8 **ounces Swiss cheese, grated**

Sprinkle each cheese over half the casserole so the two colors are side by side. Bake at 350° for 45 minutes.

Serves 6–8

CHOCOLATE POTATO CAKE

    2 cups sugar
    1 cup butter

Cream together.

    4 eggs
  ½ cup melted sweet cooking chocolate
    1 cup mashed potatoes
2½ cups sifted all-purpose flour
    2 teaspoons baking powder
  ¾ cup milk
    1 teaspoon cinnamon
    1 teaspoon nutmeg
    1 teaspoon vanilla

Add to creamed mixture in order given, sifting flour and baking powder in together. Mix thoroughly. Bake at 350° for 50 minutes in greased 1½ quart loaf pan.

Serves 6

Potatoes contribute moisture and texture to baked goods.

SWEET POTATO CASSEROLE

4–5 sweet potatoes, peeled,
     cooked, and mashed
3 egg yolks
2 tablespoons butter
3 tablespoons brown sugar
1 tablespoon baking powder
1 cup orange juice or light cream

Mix together.

3 egg whites, well beaten
½ cup chopped pecans

Fold into potatoes. Place in buttered casserole or ring. Bake 35 to 45 minutes at 350°.

Serves 8

GLAZED SWEET POTATOES

8 medium sweet potatoes, peeled

Parboil 10 to 15 minutes and slice $1/2$ inch thick. Arrange in large shallow buttered dish.

1 cup brown sugar
2 tablespoons cornstarch
$1/2$ cup raisins
$1/2$ teaspoon grated orange rind
$1/2$ teaspoon salt
2 cups orange juice

In saucepan, mix and cook about 5 minutes to thicken. Remove from heat.

$1/3$ cup butter
$1/3$ cup sherry
$1/3$ cup minced walnuts

Stir into saucepan until butter melts. Pour over potatoes. Bake at 325° for 30 minutes, basting occasionally.

Serves 8

SPINACH

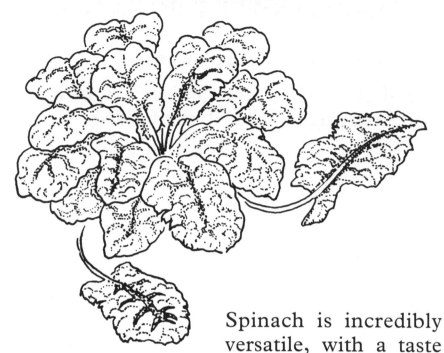

Spinach is incredibly versatile, with a taste more delicate and subtle than the other leafy greens, and a favorite base for a number of ethnic dishes. The Italians use it as a bed for eggs, sole, or veal, for stuffing ravioli or cannelloni, and for making green noodles. The Greeks use spinach in a layered strudel pie. And the French make creamed spinach, perhaps the classic of the creamed vegetables.

Spinach is most likely to have a sticky reputation in gardening circles, as it is very particular about the climate. For this reason, many home gardeners rely on New Zealand spinach, which tastes like spinach with fleshy leaves, but belongs to a different family. It is valuable, for it grows in summer weather where spinach will not. However, New Zealand spinach grows rampantly and reseeds with abandon. Be sure you like it when you plant it!

Spinach is extremely high in iron, calcium, and vitamins. Raw spinach is, like other greens, considered roughage, since the stem disposes of most of the bulk. The French call spinach a "stomach broom."

The Growing Spinach is an annual never found growing wild. It may have smooth or crinkled leaves. The plant, which grows in a bunch resembling the foliage on a violet, reaches a breadth of 8 to 10 inches. It requires 45 days of cool weather, never over 75°. Spinach goes to seed immediately when the weather warms. It is totally discriminating about the soil as well. It will bolt if the soil has too much clay or is too sandy. The plants must be kept watered or the leaves will become tough. Sow seeds ½ inch deep in rows spaced 1 inch apart. Drop about 6–8 seeds per foot. Thin later to space plants every 4 to 5 inches. Harvest the spinach about 1½ months after sowing.

The Harvest The outer leaves of the spinach plant may be cut several times while the plant is growing. This small harvest may be adequate for salads. When the plant is mature, uproot it. Spinach is essentially a one-crop vegetable.

The Basics
1 pound = 2 three inch bunches = 8 cups raw =

1½ cups cooked = 3–4 servings.
1 cup chopped raw spinach (3.5 ounces) = 26 calories, 4.3 grams carbohydrates, 3.2 grams protein, 2 times recommended daily vitamin A, more than the recommended daily vitamin C, iron and minerals, especially potassium.
½ cup cooked spinach (3.5 ounces) = 21 calories, 3.2 grams carbohydrates, 2.7 grams protein, 1½ times recommended daily vitamin A, less than recommended vitamin C, great iron and mineral loss.
10-foot row = 3 pounds spinach.

The Storage Rinse quickly. Drain and dry, but not thoroughly. Store in plastic bag in the crisper drawer for 1 or 2 days. The spinach will wilt and toughen after that.

Freezing Clean. Scald 1½ minutes. Chill in ice water. Drain. Chop if desired. Package with water that clings. Label and freeze. Cook before defrosting — probably not much extra water will be needed.

The Cooking Wash thoroughly. Several waters may be necessary. Remove stems. Some cooks prefer a great deal of cooking water, which reduces some of the acidic content. Other cooks prefer to steam the spinach in a covered skillet with little more than the rinse water clinging to the leaves.

Basic Preparation Boil 5 minutes. Serve with butter and lemon juice or butter and a few drops of vinegar.

Complementary Herbs Basil, curry, dill weed, garlic, oregano, parsley, and tarragon.

GREEN GARDEN DIP

1 cup chopped cooked spinach
1 cup mayonnaise
1 cup sour cream
½ cup minced chives or green onion
½ cup minced fresh parsley
¼ teaspoon dried dill weed
½ teaspoon salt
Fresh lemon to taste

Combine and chill.

3 cups

Serve with sliced carrots, zucchini sticks, and cherry tomatoes. Raw spinach, cut into fine slivers, works too.

CREAM OF SPINACH SOUP

3   **tablespoons butter**
2   **tablespoons flour**
1   **teaspoon salt**
$1/_8$ **teaspoon freshly ground pepper**

Melt butter, stir in flour and seasonings, and cook about 3 minutes.

1   **cup cooked spinach**
2   **cups light cream**
2   **cups beef consommé**
1   **teaspoon grated onion**

Purée in blender. Add and heat gently. Do not boil.

Serves 4-5

Grate parsley and finely mince raw spinach on top for texture.

POPEYE'S SOUP

¾ **cup minced ham**
2 **cloves garlic, minced**
3 **tablespoons oil**

Sauté in large saucepan.

1 **cup tomatoes, peeled and cubed**
2 **cups chopped spinach**
½ **teaspoon nutmeg**
4 **cups chicken broth**

Add. Cover and simmer 20 minutes.

½ **cup uncooked macaroni**

Add and continue cooking about 15 minutes, until tender.

Serves 6–8

SPANAKOPITTA

8 cups chopped spinach
1 onion, minced
4 tablespoons butter

Sauté 4 to 5 minutes.

2 tablespoons flour
1 cup milk

Stir in flour, then gradually add milk and stir until thickened. Remove from heat.

5 eggs, beaten
1 pound feta cheese, crumbled (or
other mild white cheese, grated)
Dash of nutmeg and cinnamon

Stir in until smooth.

8 ounces phyllo pastry sheets
½ cup butter, melted

In 11-by-14-inch sheet pan, brush and layer 8 sheets with butter. Add filling and repeat with 8 more layers. Bake at 350° for 30 minutes. Cut into squares.

Serves 12–18

Cut this Greek delicacy into small squares and serve as hot hors d'oeuvre. Remember, when working with phyllo, to keep unused pastry sheets moist by covering with a clamp towel.

SPINACH SALAD

4–5 cups torn spinach

Rinse, wrap in paper towels, and chill.

8 slices bacon

Fry and crumble.

2 red apples

Core and dice — don't peel.

$1/_3$ cup slivered almonds

Toast under broiler or in bacon grease.

$1/_4$ cup oil
3 tablespoons tarragon vinegar
$1/_8$ teaspoon salt
$1/_2$ teaspoon dry mustard

Mix, then toss with spinach, bacon, apples, and almonds.

Serves 6

Red apple skins and dark green spinach provide a feast for sight as well as taste.

WILTED SPINACH

4 slices bacon

Cook. Reserve 3 tablespoons grease, and crumble bacon. Set aside.

2 medium onions, sliced
7–8 cups chopped spinach
½ cup minced fresh parsley
½ teaspoon dried rosemary
1 teaspoon salt
¼ teaspoon pepper

Cook in bacon grease, covered, over medium heat 4 to 5 minutes, until wilted.

2 tablespoons wine vinegar

Add, toss in bacon, and serve.

Serves 6

SPINACH CRÊPES

  1 **cup cooked chopped spinach**
  2 **cups milk**
 ¼ **teaspoon salt**
  1 **teaspoon lemon juice**
  3 **eggs**
1½ **cups sifted flour**
  2 **tablespoons melted butter**

Purée in blender. Let sit 1 hour. Heat 8-inch greased skillet. Pour in 3 tablespoons batter and swirl batter to cover pan. Cook over medium high heat about 3 minutes. Stack finished crêpes in warm oven, then fold in quarters or roll up with filling.

Serves 6 (20-24 crêpes)

Crêpes may be filled with Monterey Jack cheese, creamed chicken, sautéed tomatoes and sour cream, or sautéed mushrooms and onions.

SPINACH RING

3 tablespoons butter
1 tablespoon chopped onion

Sauté until soft.

3 tablespoons flour

Add and cook, stirring, until smooth.

1 cup light cream

Add and stir until thickened.

1 cup chopped cooked spinach

Add and stir.

2 egg yolks
Freshly ground pepper to taste
¼ teaspoon nutmeg

Pour ½ cup spinach into yolks, stirring, then mix well with rest of spinach. Season.

3 egg whites, stiffly beaten

Fold into spinach. Pour into greased ring mold. Place in a pan of hot water. Bake at 325° for 30 minutes.

Serves 4–6

Invert this green ring and fill center with creamed mushrooms or creamed chicken.

CREAMED SPINACH

1½ cups chopped cooked spinach
¼ cup sour cream
2 tablespoons grated horseradish
2 tablespoons butter
½ teaspoon dried tarragon or nutmeg
½ teaspoon salt
Pepper to taste

Combine and heat.

Serves 3–4

Townsends Restaurant in San Francisco was famous for this.

ZUCCHINI-SPINACH FRITTATA

1 **medium onion, finely chopped**
¼ **teaspoon dried basil**
¼ **teaspoon dried rosemary**
2 **tablespoons butter**

Sauté.

1 **cup chopped cooked spinach**
6 **zucchini, cooked and drained**

Combine in a bowl and mash together.

5 **eggs, beaten**
4 **tablespoons grated Parmesan cheese**
2 **tablespoons bread crumbs**
1¼ **teaspoons salt**
¼ **teaspoon pepper**

Stir into vegetable mixture. And sautéed onions. Place in buttered 1½ quart dish, and bake at 350° for 30 minutes.

Serves 6–8

A fabulous picnic dish with chilled white burgundy, fresh fruit, and cookies. Or cut into squares, arrange on a platter and border with peas and onions for a party buffet.

PASTITSIO

  1 **large onion, chopped**
  1 **clove garlic, minced**
  2 **tablespoons olive oil**
1½ **pounds ground beef**

Sauté and pour off all fat.

 ¼ **teaspoon salt**
  1 **cup tomato sauce**
     Scant ¼ teaspoon cinnamon

Add to meat.

  3 **tablespoons butter**
 ¼ **cup flour**

Melt butter, stir in flour, and cook, stirring for several minutes.

  2 **cups milk**
 ½ **teaspoon salt**
     Dashes of pepper and nutmeg
 ¼ **cup grated Parmesan cheese**

Add to roux and stir until thickened.

  2 **cups uncooked elbow macaroni**

Cook in boiling salted water 10 minutes. Drain and put back in pot.

  2 **tablespoons butter**
  2 **eggs**

Add to macaroni and stir.

1½ cups cooked spinach
8 ounces cheddar cheese, grated

In greased shallow baking dish layer half the macaroni, all the meat, all the spinach, half the cheese, remaining macaroni, all the sauce, and remaining cheese. Bake at 375° for 1 hour.

Serves 6

This Greek casserole can be frozen or made the day before you need it. If heated directly from refrigerator, cook for 1½ hours.

SPINACH CANNELLONI

¾ **cup flour**
½ **teaspoon salt**
3 **eggs**
1 **cup milk**
1 **tablespoon oil**

Mix well in blender. Let stand 1 hour. Heat 8-inch greased pan over medium-high flame. Spoon about 3 tablespoons batter in and spread around. Cook about 2 minutes. Repeat, until batter is used up.

2 **cups cooked chopped spinach**
6 **green onions, chopped and**
    sautéed in 2 tablespoons butter
8 **ounces ricotta cheese**
1 **cup finely grated white cheese**

Mix, spoon into crêpes, and roll up.

2 **cups white sauce (p. 456)**
   Grated Parmesan cheese
2 **cups spaghetti sauce**

Spread an oblong greased casserole with two-thirds of the spaghetti sauce. Cover with all of the crêpes, then all of the white sauce. Pour remaining spaghetti sauce down center of dish. Sprinkle with cheese. Bake at 350° for 45 minutes.

Serves 6

An excellent blend of flavors. You can make ahead and refrigerate or freeze.

SPINACH, HAM, AND CHEESE TORTE

1 cup fine dry bread crumbs
¼ cup grated Parmesan cheese
4 tablespoons melted butter

Reserving 2 tablespoons bread crumbs, combine and press into a 10-inch pie plate or quiche dish.

1 pound ricotta cheese
¼ cup grated Parmesan cheese
2 tablespoons sour cream
2 tablespoons flour
2 eggs
1 teaspoon salt

Mix in blender or with electric beater.

1 cup chopped cooked spinach

Add spinach to half of the cheese mixture. Spread over crust.

¼-½ pound cooked ham, minced or slivered

Add to rest of cheese and spread over spinach.

Freshly ground pepper
Sour cream

Sprinkle top with reserved bread crumbs and pepper. Bake at 350° for 40 minutes. Serve immediately and pass with sour cream.

Serves 4

SPINACH QUICHE

2 tablespoons butter
2 tablespoons green onions, minced

Sauté in saucepan.

2 cups chopped spinach

Add to saucepan, cover, and simmer 5 minutes. Let cool a few minutes.

4 eggs
$^1/_4$ teaspoon nutmeg
$^1/_2$ teaspoon salt
Dash of pepper

Mix in blender.

$1^1/_4$ cups heavy cream, scalded

Add to blender along with spinach, and purée again immediately. Pour into shell.

1 quiche pastry shell (see p. 465)

$^1/_3$ cup grated Swiss cheese

Sprinkle atop. Bake at 375° for 25 to 30 minutes. Let stand 10 minutes before serving.

Serves 6

Ham, sausage, or bacon can be added for meatlovers. As is, it's a vegetarian's delight.

SQUASH

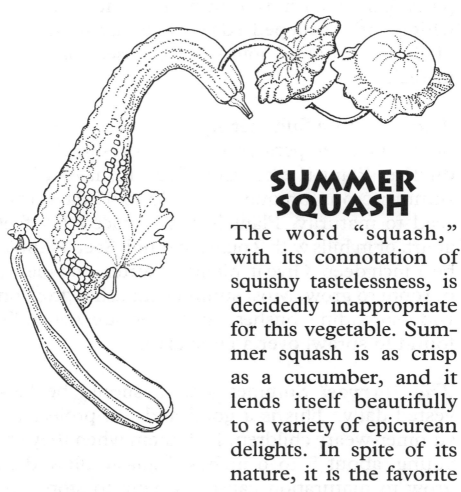

SUMMER SQUASH

The word "squash," with its connotation of squishy tastelessness, is decidedly inappropriate for this vegetable. Summer squash is as crisp as a cucumber, and it lends itself beautifully to a variety of epicurean delights. In spite of its nature, it is the favorite summer vegetable of many gardeners (at least second to tomatoes). And squash has been a favorite on this continent since the days of Indian domination, as long as 5,000 years ago.

Zucchini and cocozelle, cylindrical and light or dark green, are probably the most popular kinds. It seems odd that a native American vegetable is best known by its Italian varietal name. The yellow crookneck and straightneck squash look like they sound. All these types are interchangeable in recipes calling for summer squash. Scallop or patty pan squash is round, flat and greenish-white, with scalloped edges. It is the least tasty of the group and should not be used randomly in recipes.

The Growing Summer squash grows in a variety of summer temperatures and is tiresomely productive. Plant it early from seed to have a long summer crop. It requires only 45 to 55 days from seed to maturity. Plant in rows spaced 1½ feet apart, or in hills with 2 plants per hill. Seeds should be 1 inch deep. Give it plenty of water, and plenty of room to grow. Most summer squashes grow on wide-spreading bushes, and they are generally found to sprawl over a large area.

The Harvest Summer squash should be harvested daily. This is a good and fun project for summer-weary children. Pick them when they are young, about 5 to 6 inches. Squash allowed to grow to maturation cause the vine to stop producing. Yard-long seedy zucchini are not unusual after a week's vacation.

The Basics
1 pound = 4 medium summer squash = 2 cups sliced = 2 servings.
½ cup cooked (3.5 ounces) = 12–16 calories, 3.1 grams carbohydrates, .9 grams protein.

½ cup raw summer squash (3.5 ounces) = 19 calories, 4.2 grams carbohydrates, 1.1 grams protein.
6 plants = approximately 50 pounds.

The Storage Summer squash will keep as long as one week in the refrigerator; store it in plastic sacks. It is best cooked immediately while still crisp and full of water. Most recipes rely on fresh squash, as it does not freeze well.

Freezing Precooked squash casseroles can be frozen with moderate success. Parboiled summer squash slices may be frozen, but the results are a bit soggy. Cooked purée is the best solution (see recipe following).

The Cooking Wash squash well and cut off both ends. It does not need peeling. It may be fried, steamed, boiled, baked, or broiled. Steaming produces the crispest, least soggy result. Always parboil squash for oven casseroles, or the dish will become soupy. All recipes are based on 5- to 6-inch squash. For larger squash, reduce the number of squash.

Basic Preparation Steam whole summer squash 10 minutes, sliced squash 3 to 5 minutes. Serve with butter and lemon juice.

Complementary Herbs Basil, chili powder, curry, garlic, oregano, and parsley.

SQUASH PURÉE

3 cloves garlic, minced
3 large onions, chopped
6 tablespoons butter

Cook 5 to 10 minutes in 15-quart pot.

5 quarts chopped summer squash
2¼ teaspoons salt
1 teaspoon pepper
¼ cup water (more if necessary)
1 cup chopped fresh parsley

Add and cook covered until squash is soft. Stir often. Purée well in blender. Freeze in labeled containers.

9 pints

This purée, which freezes perfectly, can be used in a variety of casseroles and soups. Freeze the basic recipe, or preseason it for a favorite recipe.

VICHY SQUASH

1 medium onion, sliced
¼ cup butter

Sauté until transparent.

6 medium summer squash, chopped
½ cup beef or chicken broth

Add, cover, and simmer about 10 minutes until tender. Purée in blender. (Freeze, if desired, at this point.)

¼ teaspoon salt
Dash of pepper
½ cup milk
½ cup cream

Add and chill before serving.

Serves 4

Here is an elegant soup which works just as nicely with frozen purée (see preceding recipe). Serve with chopped chives, parsley, or a thin slice of lemon. For an interesting vegetable soup, toss in cooked snap beans and carrots and substitute broth for cream.

RAW SUMMER SQUASH SALAD WITH TOMATOES

1 small zucchini
1 tomato

Slice and arrange in dish.

Juice of ½ lemon
2 tablespoons olive oil
Salt and pepper to taste
2–3 leaves of minced fresh basil

Mix and drizzle over vegetables.

Serves 2

This is simple and lovely. It is best with garden-temperature zucchini and tomatoes.

ZUCCHINI IN SALSA VERDE

6 medium zucchini, sliced 1-inch thick
½ cup flour
1¾ teaspoons salt
Olive oil

Roll zucchini in flour and salt, then brown in oil.

3 tablespoons white wine vinegar
3 minced anchovies
½ clove garlic, minced
¼ cup minced fresh parsley
Juice of 1 lemon
½ teaspoon freshly ground pepper

Combine and pour over zucchini. Marinate 2 to 3 hours.

Serves 4

A super Italian first course for a summer dinner party. Serve with lemon wedges.

SWEET-AND-SOUR SQUASH

  4 **small zucchini**
  4 **small yellow squash**
  3 **stalks celery**
  1 **sweet red pepper (optional)**

Slice paper thin into large, shallow bowl.

  1 **finely chopped red onion**
  1 **cup wine vinegar**
  $^3/_4$ **cup sugar**
  $^1/_3$ **cup oil**
  1 **teaspoon salt**
  1 **teaspoon pepper**

Bring to boil to dissolve sugar. Pour over vegetables. Cover and chill at least 4 hours. Drain and serve.

Serves 6–8

Perfectly delicious when you pick the squash off the vine and prepare. Use only the freshest vegetables for raw preparations.

STEAMED SUMMER SQUASH VINAIGRETTE

6 zucchini, sliced thinly

Steam until crisp-tender. Plunge under cold water. Drain. Chill.

6 tablespoons olive oil
2 tablespoons red wine vinegar
1 tablespoon Dijon mustard (optional)
Salt and pepper to taste
1 shallot minced (optional)

Mix and pour over zucchini.

Serves 4

ZUCCHINI RELISH

10 cups finely chopped zucchini
4 cups finely chopped onion
3 cups finely chopped carrots
2 cups finely chopped green peppers
¼ cup salt

Combine and let stand 3 hours. Drain.

2 cups cider vinegar
4 cups sugar
2 tablespoons cornstarch mixed with
   water into paste
2 teaspoons celery seed
1 teaspoon black pepper
1 teaspoon turmeric
1 teaspoon nutmeg

Bring to boil in large kettle and add vegetables.
Stir constantly. Ladle into sterilized jars. Seal.

12 pints

Use on hot dogs, ham sandwiches, and salami — or just open it out of the jar.

SUMMER SQUASH PICKLES

20–30 sliced summer squash
    8 large onions, chopped
    2 large bell peppers, chopped
  ½ cup salt

Combine and let stand 3 hours. Drain.

    5 cups sugar
    5 cups cider vinegar
    2 tablespoons mustard seed
  ½ tablespoon ground cloves
    1 teaspoon turmeric

Combine and bring to boil. Add vegetables. Do not boil. Put in sterilized jars and seal.

12 pints

SAUTÉED SUMMER SQUASH

3-4 tablespoons olive oil
4 zucchini, sliced

Heat oil. Sauté zucchini 2 minutes over high heat, browning on both sides. Do not overcook.

1 clove garlic, minced
Grated Parmesan cheese
Salt and pepper to taste

Turn off heat and stir in fresh garlic. Sprinkle with Parmesan and seasonings.

Serves 3-4

Butter or bacon grease can be substituted for olive oil. In that case, omit cheese and garlic. This dish is quickly prepared and an ideal accompaniment to barbecued meat.

BROILED SUMMER SQUASH

4 summer squash

Parboil 6 minutes, drain, and cut into halves lengthwise. Score tops with sharp knife.

> **Butter**
> **Celery salt**
> **Bread crumbs**
> **Grated Parmesan cheese**

Coat with a layer of each in order given. Broil a few minutes to brown cheese.

Serves 4

STEAMED SHREDDED
SUMMER SQUASH

6 medium summer squash, grated

Put in hot pan and cover for 2 minutes. Stir. With cover off, heat 2 minutes more, letting moisture evaporate. It should be crisp.

½–1 lemon
Salt and pepper to taste

Squeeze lemon juice over. Season.

Serves 4–6

Surprisingly different. Your calorie counter will love it. Even butterholics will ask for more. You can vary recipe by sautéing grated carrots with squash.

SEVEN-MINUTE ZUCCHINI

4 medium zucchini, grated
1 teaspoon salt

Combine and let stand.

½ pound mushrooms

Heat mushrooms in skillet, shaking over high heat until liquid evaporates.

¼ cup butter
¼ cup sliced green onions
1 clove minced garlic

Add to skillet and sauté. Squeeze excess liquid out of zucchini. Add to onions and mushrooms and stir occasionally over heat for 5 minutes.

½ cup sour cream
1 tablespoon chopped fresh basil

Stir in, heat, and serve.

Serves 3–4

BEEF ZUCCHINI RATATOUILLE

2 **large onions, diced**
2 **tablespoons olive oil**

Sauté 5 minutes.

4 **zucchini, thinly sliced**
6 **tomatoes, peeled and sliced**
1 **small to medium eggplant, peeled and diced**
1 **green pepper, diced**
1 **clove garlic, minced**

Add to onions and cook 30 minutes, stirring occasionally.

1–1½ **pounds ground chuck**
½ **teaspoon salt**

Brown meat, drain, and add to vegetables. Cook 5 minutes more. Season.

Serves 4

Substitute ground lamb for variation.

SUMMER SQUASH PANCAKES

   3 **cups grated squash**
  ½ **teaspoon salt**
   3 **teaspoons minced fresh parsley**
   1 **clove garlic, minced**
  ¾ **cup grated Parmesan cheese**
   1 **egg**
¾–1 **cup biscuit mix**
      Dash of pepper

Mix to make a fairly thin batter. Drop by spoonfuls into oiled skillet. Cook. Turn once when golden. May be reheated in oven.

Serves 8

CURRIED LAMB WITH ZUCCHINI

2½ tablespoons butter
1 onion, chopped
1 green pepper, thinly sliced
1 clove garlic, mashed

Sauté until glossy in large skillet.

3–4 zucchini, sliced

Add and sauté for 5 minutes.

1 cup chicken stock
2 tablespoons soy sauce
2 teaspoons dry mustard
⅓–½ cup apricot preserves
1–2 teaspoons curry powder

Stir into skillet.

1 tablespoon cornstarch dissolved in
2 tablespoons water

Stir in to thicken.

2–3 cups cubed, cooked lamb

Add to skillet and heat.

1 avocado, sliced

Add and serve.

Serves 4

A good choice for leftover leg of lamb. Serve with rice garnished with almonds, sliced tomatoes and marinated cucumbers.

SUMMER SQUASH
FRITTATA CASSEROLE

4–5 **cups shredded zucchini**
   1 **teaspoon salt**

Combine and let stand 30 minutes to 3 hours. Drain.

$1/4$ **cup biscuit mix**
$1/4$ **cup minced fresh parsley**
1–2 **green onions, minced**
$1/8$ **teaspoon pepper**
$1/2$ **clove minced garlic**
   4 **eggs, well beaten**

Add to zucchini and stir just until well blended.

   2 **tablespoons butter**

Pour mixture into buttered casserole, dot with butter, and bake uncovered at 350° for 25 minutes or until set.

Serves 6

Frittata can be an appetizer, cut into cubes; a lunch, cut into wedges; an entrée accompanied by freshly steamed vegetables and fruit.

SUMMER SQUASH RING

6   summer squash, cooked and
      mashed or puréed
6   green onions, minced and sautéed
6   slices bread, shredded
¼   cup grated Parmesan cheese
1   cup milk
3   tablespoons chopped fresh basil
1   tablespoon chopped fresh parsley
½   teaspoon salt
¼   teaspoon pepper
3   eggs, beaten

Mix well. Pour into greased ring mold, place pan
in hot water, and bake at 350° for 45 minutes.

Serves 6

*Don't hesitate to use frozen squash purée (see p. 348)
for this, although the fresh parboiled, finely chopped
squash has a lovely texture. A pretty mold, this ring
looks good on a buffet table. To serve, fill center with
peas, onions, artichoke hearts, or creamed chicken.*

GREEN AND GOLD
SUMMER SQUASH

2 tablespoons olive oil
1 onion, minced

Sauté.

3 zucchini, grated
3 yellow crookneck squash, grated
¼ cup fresh parsley, minced
½ teaspoon dried oregano
½ teaspoon salt
½ teaspoon pepper
3 eggs, slightly beaten
½ cup milk

Stir into onions until blended. Pour half into a buttered 1½-quart casserole.

1 cup grated Monterey Jack cheese
½ cup crushed soda crackers

Sprinkle half of each over squash and then repeat layers. Bake at 350° for 30 minutes, until bubbly.

Serves 6

ZUCCHINI CRÊPES

5–6 zucchini, shredded
1 teaspoon salt

Mix and let stand in colander 30 minutes. Drain, and press out water.

5 eggs
$^2/_3$ cup milk
2 minced green onions
1 clove garlic, minced
$^3/_4$ teaspoon baking powder
Dash of Tabasco

Purée in blender, then stir in zucchini. Fry $^1/_4$ cup batter at a time, spreading it out, in buttered 8-inch pan over high heat. (Freeze, if desired, at this point.)

2 cups ricotta cheese
1 cup grated Monterey Jack or similar white cheese
1 cup grated Parmesan cheese
Dash of salt

Mix well, fill crêpes, and roll up. Bake in 400° oven about 10 minutes, until cheese melts.

Serves 8

ENCHILADAS DE ZUCCHINI

1 dozen corn tortillas

Fry each tortilla 2 minutes in hot oil, until heated through but still pliable. Drain on paper towels.

2 tablespoons oil
1 pound lean ground beef
1 yellow onion, minced

Sauté 10 minutes. Drain off grease.

3–4 cups zucchini, grated
**1 small can green olives, drained
   and chopped**

Add and sauté 5 minutes more. Spoon the sauce into the 12 tortillas.

2 cups Monterey Jack cheese, grated

Sprinkle atop the sauce and then roll the tortillas up and place in a shallow baking dish.

**2½ cups (3 seven-ounce cans)
   enchilada sauce**

Pour over tortillas.

Monterey Jack cheese, grated

Sprinkle with cheese and bake at 350° for 15 minutes. If refrigerated, bake 30 minutes.

Serves 6

Están muy delicioso! The enchiladas may be prepared ahead of time and refrigerated before baking.

CALABACITAS

3 large or 6 small zucchini

Parboil about 10 minutes until fork-tender. Drain, slice in halves lengthwise, and scoop pulp into a bowl, reserving shells.

$1/_2$ onion, finely minced
1 tablespoon butter

Sauté onion in butter.

$1/_2$ pound Monterey Jack cheese, grated
$1/_8$ teaspoon salt

Mix with onions and zucchini pulp.

6 soda crackers, crushed

Stuff mixture into shells and sprinkle with crackers. Bake at 350° for 15 to 20 minutes. Broil tops until golden.

Serves 6

Add 1 cup cottage cheese and there is enough protein in this Mexican dish for the main course.

ZUCCHINI PIZZA

Crust

4 ounces Mozzarella cheese
4 ounces cheddar cheese
4 cups grated zucchini
2 eggs
2 tablespoons biscuit mix
¼ teaspoon salt

Combine all and press into a 10 by 15 inch jelly roll pan. Bake at 400° for 15 minutes.

Topping

2 tablespoons oil
1 onion, minced
1 clove garlic, minced
1 pound ground beef

Sauté 10 minutes. Drain off fat.

1 cup tomato sauce
   Salt and pepper to taste
1 teaspoon oregano

Stir into meat. Spoon over baked crust.

2 ounces Mozzarella cheese
2 ounces cheddar cheese

Grate over meat. Bake at 400° for 20 minutes.

Serves 6–8

ZUCCHINI BREAD

  3 **cups grated zucchini**
  1 **cup oil**
1½ **cups sugar**
  3 **eggs, beaten**
  1 **teaspoon vanilla**

Combine.

  3 **cups flour**
1½ **teaspoons baking powder**
  1 **teaspoon soda**
1½ **teaspoons cinnamon**
  1 **teaspoon salt**
  ½ **teaspoon ginger**

Sift in together, and stir to blend.

  1 **cup chopped nuts**
  1 **cup raisins**

Add, and beat 4 minutes. Place in greased loaf pan and bake 1 hour at 350°.

1 large loaf

When the squash loads up in the refrigerator, put aside a couple of hours and make loaves to freeze. You might make zucchini cookies or zucchini chocolate cake (see following recipes) to freeze at the same time.

ZUCCHINI DROP COOKIES

1 cup grated zucchini
1 teaspoon soda
1 cup sugar
½ cup shortening or butter
1 egg beaten

Mix together.

2 cups flour
1 teaspoon cinnamon
½ teaspoon ground cloves
½ teaspoon salt

Sift in and stir to blend.

1 cup chopped nuts
1 cup raisins

Stir in, then drop batter by teaspoonfuls on greased cookie sheet. Bake 12 to 15 minutes at 375°.

3 dozen

These are like hermits, but better.

TOO-BIG-TO-COOK
STUFFED SQUASH

Here are some ideas for the oversized summer squash. (If they are longer than a foot, toss them in the compost heap.) Half the fun is creating your own delicacy with whatever you would like to get rid of. Don't be afraid to experiment.

Large squash, halved

Parboil until just tender. Scoop out and discard pithy part and seeds. Fill cavity with any of the following and bake at 350° until thoroughly heated.

Spaghetti Stuffing

Cooked ground beef and spaghetti sauce with a slice of mozzarella broiled on top.

Ham Stuffing

Minced, cooked ham, French bread crumbs, dry mustard, minced onion, moistened with broth or béchamel sauce.

Hamburger Rice Stuffing

Cooked ground beef with cooked brown rice, green onions, water, broiled with Parmesan cheese.

Spinach and Sausage Stuffing

Cooked sausage and seasoned bread crumbs, eggs, green pepper, onions, and cooked spinach.

Pizza Stuffing

Chopped salami or bologna, grated Mozzarella cheese, onions, bread crumbs, tomato sauce.

Chinese Pork Stuffing

Cooked pork, cooked white rice, soy sauce, sherry, sugar, chopped scallions.

Spanish Rice Stuffing

Spanish rice mix, cooked ground beef, tomatoes.

Greek Stuffing

Cooked ground or cubed lamb, cooked brown rice, minced garlic, a squeeze of lcmon.

Chard Stuffing

Cooked chard, white sauce, nutmeg, Swiss cheese.

ZUCCHINI GOULASH

1 large onion, diced
¼ pound mushrooms, sliced
2 tablespoons olive oil

Using a large pot, sauté until soft.

1 pound ground chuck

Add; cook until crumbly.

1½ teaspoons paprika
¼ cup minced green pepper
2 tablespoons fresh minced parsley
¾ teaspoon salt
¼ teaspoon pepper
2 teaspoons minced fresh basil
2 cups peeled, diced tomatoes

Add, cover, and simmer 15 minutes.

6 zucchini, sliced diagonally

Add to skillet; stir well, cover, and simmer 20 minutes, until tender.

Grated Parmesan cheese

Serve in bowls and sprinkle with cheese.

Serves 4

ZUCCHINI FRITTERS

4–6 zucchini
1 tablespoon salt

Cut zucchini in fingers 3 by ½ by ½ inches. Add salt. Let stand 20 minutes. Drain.

½ cup flour
1 egg
1 teaspoon baking powder
2 tablespoons milk (or more)

Mix. Dip zucchini fingers in batter.

Oil for deep frying

Fry in hot oil until brown on all sides. Drain.

Lemon wedges

Serve hot with lemon.

Serves 4–6

Zucchini fritters are a wonderful hors d'oeuvre. Cook plenty. Cocktail guests can't get enough. May be made ahead and reheated at 375° 5 to 10 minutes.

CHOCOLATE ZUCCHINI CAKE

  1 **cup brown sugar**
  ½ **cup white sugar**
  ½ **cup butter**
  ½ **cup oil**

Cream together in large bowl.

  3 **eggs**
  1 **teaspoon vanilla**
  ½ **cup buttermilk**

Add and stir well to mix.

 2½ **cups flour**
  ½ **teaspoon allspice**
  ½ **teaspoon cinnamon**
  ½ **teaspoon salt**
  2 **teaspoons baking soda**
  4 **tablespoons cocoa**

Measure into sifter, then sift into bowl.

  3 **zucchini, approximately 6 inches long**

Grate into the bowl. Stir until blended. Pour into greased, floured 9-by-13-inch pan.

½-1 **cup chocolate chips**

Sprinkle on top. Bake at 325° for 45 minutes.

Very moist and delicious. A good choice for a family outing. Friends will never guess the ingredients.

ZUCCHINI-GRANOLA COOKIES

¾ cup butter
1½ cups brown sugar
1 egg
1 teaspoon vanilla
Grated rind of 1 orange
3 cups grated zucchini

Cream butter and sugar. Combine with other ingredients in a large bowl.

3–3½ cups flour
1 teaspoon soda
1 teaspoon salt

Sift into zucchini mixture.

3 cups granola cereal
1 cup butterscotch chips or
chocolate chips

Stir in. Dough should be sticky. Drop by spoonfuls on cookie sheet. Bake at 350° for 12 to 15 minutes.

Makes 6 dozen

WINTER SQUASH

Cooked winter squash has a consistency something like mashed potatoes, so the word "squash" is quite appropriate in this instance. Winter squash have a yellow-orange flesh, although the exteriors come in many shapes, sizes, and colors. Pumpkins are frequently included in the group of winter squash, since they share this group's growing characteristics. Other varieties of winter squash include Hubbard, which grows to 10 to 15 pounds, banana, butternut, and acorn or Danish.

The Growing Most winter squashes are non-climbing vine plants and thus require a lot of room. They require 75 to 120 days to mature, depending on variety: acorn squash matures the earliest; Hubbard takes longest. It is possible to grow squash vines at the base of corn to utilize ground space. The Indians grew pumpkins in this manner. Plant seeds 1 inch deep with 2 plants per group. Allow 10 feet between groups so vines can ramble.

The Harvest Winter squash are usually allowed to ripen on the vine. Let the rinds get very hard and the squash heavy. Cut the stem with 1 or 2 inches attached. If the stem is cut at the base, the squash will rot at that point. Squash can cure for about one week in the sun after harvesting.

The Basics
1 pound = 1 six-inch acorn squash = 2 cups peeled and diced.
1 pound = ½ eight-inch butternut squash = 2 cups peeled and diced.
½ cup cooked winter squash (3.5 ounces) = 63 calories, 15.4 grams carbohydrates, 1.2 grams protein, high vitamin A content.
1 hill winter squash = 30 pounds.

The Storage Winter squash is one of the few vegetables that do not lose any quality after picking. During storage, in fact, the carotenoid content increases, adding to the vitamin A content.

Store squash in a cool, dark place. The Hubbard will store this way for as long as four months. After the squash is cut, it does not need refrigeration. The cut pieces should be wrapped in plastic and will last five days in a cool place.

Freezing Squash purée may be frozen. Quarter a squash. Remove seeds and stringy top layer. Dice the quarters into large pieces and then peel all. Put into a large heavy pot with about 1 cup of water (it doesn't need to cover squash, as they are juicy). Cover pot and cook over medium heat 20 to 30 minutes, or until soft. Drain off water and purée in blender or push through strainer or food mill. Freeze in bags and label.

The Cooking Winter squash may be baked whole or in pieces, or boiled. Cooked mashed squash seasoned with brown sugar and butter is excellent served in the same manner as mashed potatoes. Bake the smaller squashes whole (skin should be washed, pricked and lightly oiled). Bake at 425° for 45 minutes to 1 hour. Cut larger squash in portions, remove seeds, cover with foil, or invert on an oiled baking sheet, and bake at 350° for 1 hour. Serve squash with butter, salt and freshly ground pepper. Squash seeds, especially pumpkin, are good roasted on cookie sheets at 350° for 20 minutes.

Complementary Herbs Cinnamon, cloves, and nutmeg.

SQUASH AND APPLE SOUP

1 medium winter squash

Bake at 425° until done, 45 minutes to 1 hour. Halve, remove pulp and seeds.

3 tart green apples, chopped
1 onion, chopped
$1/_4$ teaspoon dried rosemary
$1/_4$ teaspoon dried marjoram
4 cups chicken broth
1 teaspoon salt
$1/_8$ teaspoon pepper
$1/_4$ teaspoon curry

Combine and simmer 45 minutes. Add squash pulp. Blend well in blender. Reheat before serving.

Serves 6

Serve hot with fresh parsley on top. A nice first course; also good for a casual meal of cold cuts, French bread, and butter.

WINTER SQUASH
WITH CURRIED FRUIT

2–3 acorn squash or 1 medium winter squash peeled and sliced 1-inch thick

Arrange in buttered oblong baking dish.

1 cup sliced apples
1 cup sliced peaches
1 cup apricot halves

Arrange on top of squash.

$^1/_3$ cup melted butter
$^3/_4$ cup brown sugar
1 tablespoon curry powder

Mix and pour over. Cover with foil and bake at 350° for about 40 minutes.

Serves 4

Serve with thick slices of grilled ham and a lettuce salad with mustard vinaigrette.

SQUASH WITH SAUSAGE

3 pounds winter squash

Cut squash in half. Discard seeds, invert on baking sheet and bake in 350° oven for 30 to 40 minutes.

1 pound cooked ground pork sausage
1 cup finely chopped celery
½ cup sliced mushrooms
1 cup finely chopped onion

Sauté for 7 minutes.

1 egg, beaten
½ cup sour cream
¼ cup grated mild cheese
¼ teaspoon salt

Combine and add to meat. Fill squash cavities and bake in 350° oven for 15 minutes.

Serves 4

LAMB AND
WINTER SQUASH STEW

2 pounds lamb stewing meat
Flour
½ cup olive oil

Dredge meat with flour and brown in Dutch oven.
Pour off all but 2 tablespoons fat.

¾ minced onion

Sauté until soft in same pot.

¾ teaspoon cinnamon
½ teaspoon ground cardamom
½ teaspoon ground ginger
¼ teaspoon allspice
¼ teaspoon minced garlic
Pinch of cayenne pepper

Add to pot and mix well.

2 cups beef broth

Add to pot and simmer covered 1 hour.

2 cups cooked, cubed winter squash

Add and simmer covered 15 minutes.

1½ tablespoons cornstarch
3 tablespoons orange juice

Dissolve cornstarch in orange juice. Add to stew.
Stir until thickened.

Serves 4

Serve this spicy stew over brown rice.

WINTER SQUASH
WITH ORANGE SAUCE

4 **cups cooked and mashed winter squash**
2 **tablespoons butter**
2 **tablespoons cream**
$^1/_2$ **teaspoon salt**
Pepper to taste

Mix well. Pour into buttered casserole.

2 **large oranges, grated rind and juice**
1 **tablespoon cornstarch**
$^1/_3$ **cup brown sugar**

Stir over low heat until thickened.

$^1/_4$ **cup butter**

Stir into sauce. Pour over squash. Bake at 350° for 20 minutes.

Serves 4

The sauce keeps the squash purée moist. A good choice in fall when the nights get frosty.

STUFFED ACORN SQUASH

3 acorn squash

Halve and scrape out seeds. Invert on baking sheet and bake 30 to 40 minutes at 350°.

> **Salt**
> **¼ cup butter**

Turn squash cut side up and sprinkle in cavities.

> **1 apple, diced**
> **1½ cups pineapple tidbits, drained (reserve liquid)**
> **¼ cup raisins**
> **2 tablespoons brown sugar**

Mix and fill squash cavities. Continue baking for 30 minutes. Baste with pineapple juice while baking.

Serves 6

Also good filled with creamed onions. May be prepared ahead and chilled until ready to bake.

SQUASH SOUFFLÉ

3 cups mashed cooked squash
4 tablespoons butter
2 tablespoons brown sugar
$1/_2$ teaspoon grated orange peel
$1/_8$ teaspoon ground nutmeg
$1/_2$ teaspoon salt
Dash of pepper

Mix and beat until blended.

4 egg yolks

Add and beat well.

4 egg whites

Beat until stiff. Fold into squash mixture and place in 6-cup buttered soufflé dish. Bake in 350° oven for 55 to 60 minutes.

Serves 8

EASY SQUASH CAKE

$2^1/_2$ cups flour
   4 teaspoons baking powder
 $^1/_2$ teaspoon salt
   1 teaspoon cinnamon
 $^1/_4$ teaspoon ground cloves

Put all in a sifter.

 $^1/_2$ cup shortening
$1^1/_2$ cups sugar
   3 eggs

Beat until fluffy. Sift in dry ingredients and mix until blended.

 $^1/_3$ cup milk
   1 cup puréed squash

Stir in until well blended. Bake at 350° in greased 9-by-13-inch pan 25 to 30 minutes.

Serves 6

WINTER SQUASH DOUGHNUTS

1¼ **cups sugar**
2 **tablespoons shortening**

Cream together.

2 **eggs, beaten**
1 **cup mashed cooked squash**
1 **teaspoon vanilla**

Beat into mixture.

3 **cups flour**
3 **teaspoons baking powder**
½ **teaspoon salt**
½ **teaspoon nutmeg**
½ **teaspoon cinnamon**

1 **cup milk**

Add milk and dry ingredients alternately to mixture. Chill. Roll ¼-inch thick and cut.

Oil for deep frying
Confectioner's sugar

Fry doughnuts in oil at 365° until brown. Drain. Dust with sugar.

3 dozen

A fun treat.

WINTER SQUASH PIE

¾ **cup light-brown sugar**
1 **envelope plain gelatin**
1 **teaspoon cinnamon**
½ **teaspoon cloves**
½ **teaspoon salt**
¼ **teaspoon nutmeg**

Combine in large saucepan.

3 **egg yolks**
½ **cup milk**
3 **cups puréed squash**

Add to saucepan. Cook over medium heat, stirring constantly, about 8 minutes. Cool slightly.

½ **pint sour cream**

Add and beat well.

3 **egg whites**
¼ **cup sugar**

Beat egg whites, gradually adding sugar. Fold into squash mixture.

Two 9-inch baked pie shells

Pour into baked shells. Chill 4 hours.

Serves 12

PUMPKIN CHIFFON PIE

3 egg whites
½ cup sugar

Beat until stiff, adding sugar gradually. Chill.

½ cup sugar
3 egg yolks
1½ cups puréed pumpkin
½ cup milk
½ teaspoon salt
½ teaspoon nutmeg
½ teaspoon ginger
½ teaspoon cinnamon
¼ teaspoon ground cloves

Put in top of double boiler. Mix. Stir frequently and cook until thickened. Remove from heat.

1 envelope gelatin dissolved in
¼ cup cold water

Stir into pumpkin mixture and chill. When mixture begins to thicken well, fold in egg whites.

1 graham cracker crust

Pour into shell and chill.

Whipped cream

Top with whipped cream.

Serves 6

The best of all pumpkin pies!

TRADITIONAL PUMPKIN PIE

3 eggs
$2/_3$ cup sugar (brown or white, or both)
$1^1/_2$ cups milk or cream
$1/_2$ teaspoon ginger
1 teaspoon cinnamon
$1/_2$ teaspoon salt
1 teaspoon vanilla
$1^1/_2$ cups puréed pumpkin

Mix in order given.

Two 8-inch pie shells

Pour into pie shells and bake at 450° for 15 minutes, then at 325° for 30 minutes.

Whipped cream

Cool pies, then top with whipped cream.

Serves 12

PUMPKIN BREAD

¹/₂ medium pumpkin

Quarter and steam until soft. Mash the meat — discarding skin. Measure out 2 cups.

3¹/₂ cups flour
2 teaspoons soda
¹/₂ teaspoon salt
1 teaspoon cinnamon
1 teaspoon nutmeg
3 cups sugar

Mix and make a well in center.

1 cup oil
4 eggs
²/₃ cup water

Add in center along with mashed pumpkin and stir just until all is mixed in. Pour into 1 large and 2 small oiled bread pans. Bake at 350° for 1 hour.

3 loaves

Pumpkin bread is an old favorite that keeps for weeks wrapped in foil and refrigerated. For the holidays serve the bread with a frosting made with 3 ounces cream cheese, juice of 1 orange, and the grated rind of ¹/₂ orange. Or make in the fall and freeze for Christmas presents. Any squash may be substituted.

TOMATOES

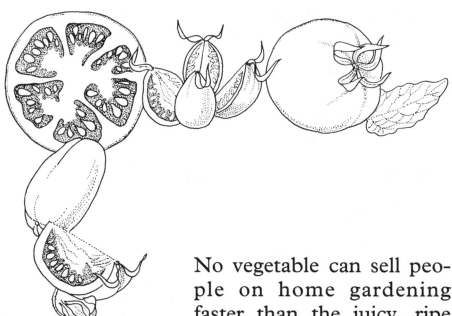

No vegetable can sell people on home gardening
faster than the juicy, ripe
tomato. Simply everyone
loves vine-ripened toma-
toes. They are easy to grow,
productive, and delicious.
Yet as much as our nation now craves fresh tomatoes, our ancestors found them unappetizing.
Historians have queried this phenomenon and
suppose the disfavor was due to folklore. Thomas
Jefferson recorded planting and eating tomatoes
at a time when many Americans considered them
poisonous. The tomato is native to Peru and was
brought north by Mexican Indians.

The big, red, round tomato is the most familiar and probably the best for slicing. Tomatoes, however, come in many colors and sizes. They can be orange, orange-pink, yellow, and even green when ripe. Sizes range from the very small cherry tomato to a mid-sized oval tomato used for tomato paste to the giants at two pounds. Plant the variety you prefer and one that is compatible with the climate and resistant to wilt and other disease.

The Growing Tomatoes thrive on warm weather and lots of sunshine. Seed inside during early spring or buy transplants. Select varieties with a built-in resistance to verticillium wilt and fusarium wilt, widespread tomato diseases. Plants will be marked V-F resistant. Transplant seedlings deeply, up to the first leaves. Mulch to prevent blossom-end rot. Set plants at 3-foot intervals in rows spaced 3 feet apart. Fruit failure may be caused by cool weather, too much or too little water, lack of fertilizer, or too much shade. The vines may be allowed to ramble on the ground or supported on a single stake, a pair of stakes, or a tepee (three stakes), or surrounded with a circle of chicken wire. Once established, water deeply at the base of the plant every 4 to 6 days. Do not water overhead. Tomatoes require 50 to 75 days to mature from seed, about 45 days from transplanted seedlings.

The Harvest Keep picked for high yield. The color indicates the ripeness.

The Basics

1 pound = 2 four-inch tomatoes = 1¼ cups sliced = 2 servings.

1 small tomato (3.5 ounces) = 22 calories, 4.7 grams carbohydrates, .2 grams fat, 1.1 grams protein, 75 percent daily recommended vitamin C, good source of vitamin A (although less than most greens). Green tomatoes have much less vitamin A and more calories and carbohydrates.

10-foot row = 3 plants = 20 pounds.

The storage Store ripened tomatoes in the refrigerator for several days. They are best immediately after picking. To ripen, lay stem end down and store in a cool place (not in sunlight).

Freezing Tomatoes are high in water content and freezing changes their texture. However, firm whole tomatoes may simply be washed, wrapped in foil, and frozen, to use for cooking, within 2 months. Finely chopped fresh tomatoes may similarly be frozen in plastic sacks to use for cooking. A perfect freezer item to use up the bounty is tomato sauce.

The Cooking As fabulous as tomatoes are raw, they are just as great for seasoning many dishes. Innumerable classic dishes rely on the tomato as a key ingredient. In some cases the tomato should be peeled, seeded, and juiced. This is a simple process. Dip the tomato in boiling water for 30 seconds to 1 minute. The skin will come right off. (Sometimes this is not necessary with very ripe tomatoes.) Cut in half, and gently squeeze out the seeds and juice. Seeds and juice are removed when their bitter flavor would alter the recipe results or when the juice is not needed.

Tomatoes may be braised, stewed, fried, or baked. They do not require long cooking for basic preparation. A baked tomato is really only a heated tomato.

Complementary Herbs Basil, bay leaves, chili powder, curry, dill weed, garlic, mint, oregano, parsley, and thyme.

STUFFED CHERRY-TOMATO APPETIZERS

Cherry tomatoes
Stuffing (see below)

To prepare, slice off tops and a very thin slice off bottom so they will stand well. Squeeze gently until all seeds and juice are out. There will be 2 or 3 cavities. Gently push pulp to one side to make 1 large cavity. Salt inside. Fill with one of the stuffings below.

Smoked Oysters

Drain and stuff 1 large smoked oyster in each tomato. Squeeze small amount of lemon juice over each.

Guacamole

Mix together 1 avocado, peeled and mashed; 2 tablespoons minced onion; juice of ½ large lemon; salt and pepper to taste.

Radish Cream

Blend 3 ounces cream cheese; 2 tablespoons minced radishes; 1 tablespoon minced green onion; 1 tablespoon minced fresh parsley; 1 teaspoon lemon juice; dash of garlic salt and paprika.

Tuna

Blend 6½ ounces tuna, drained; 2 tablespoons mayonnaise; ½ teaspoon Dijon mustard; dash of freshly ground pepper.

Watercress

Mix equal amounts of minced watercress and cream cheese; season with lemon juice. Top stuffed tomato with a whole leaf of watercress.

Peanut Curry

Combine ¼ cup peanuts, pulverized in blender; 1–2 tablespoons mayonnaise; 1 teaspoon curry powder.

CHERRY TOMATOES
WITH HERB CREAM

1   cup mayonnaise
½   cup sour cream
1   teaspoon dried Italian herbs
1½ teaspoons lemon juice
½   teaspoon Worcestershire sauce
¼   teaspoon salt
1   tablespoon chopped green onion
2   teaspoons capers

Mix well. Chill to blend.

Cherry tomatoes, unstemmed

Serve in a bowl surrounded by mounds of tomatoes.

V-3 JUICE

10–12 **tomatoes, sliced**
   ¼ **cup vinegar**
   1 **teaspoon sugar**
   1 **teaspoon salt**
   1 **bay leaf**
   2 **shoots of celery leaves**
   2 **slices onion**

Bring to boil, then simmer 30 minutes. Strain and seal in sterilized pint jars or chill in refrigerator until serving.

4 cups

Pour juice into a tall glass filled with ice cubes and garnish with a celery stick. A super pick-me-up for a hot day.

VERY FRESH
CREAM OF TOMATO SOUP

12 very ripe tomatoes, peeled, cut up
1 cup water or stock
1 cup sliced celery
½ onion, sliced
¼ cup minced fresh parsley

Simmer 30 minutes. Purée and strain.

3 tablespoons cornstarch
3 tablespoons butter, melted

Mix together. Stir into soup to thicken over medium heat.

2 tablespoons brown sugar
2 teaspoons salt
Freshly ground pepper to taste

Add. (Freeze, if desired, at this point.)

2 cups light cream
1 egg yolk, beaten

Stir into very hot soup.

Serves 6–8

Much better than anybody's canned! Freeze this in bags prior to adding the cream and egg yolks, and enjoy summer-fresh cooking all winter. The frozen base is an excellent tomato sauce as well.

EGG FLOWER SOUP

4 cups chicken broth
2 ripe tomatoes, peeled,
   seeded and diced
2 green onions, sliced

Place the chicken broth in a saucepan with the tomatoes and green onions. Cover, bring to a boil, and simmer for 5 minutes.

1 egg, slightly beaten

Bring soup to a boil again, pour in egg and stir constantly about 2 minutes or until the egg separates into shreds.

Serves 6

GAZPACHO I

 6 medium tomatoes, peeled
   and chopped
 ½ cup chopped Bermuda onion
 1 green pepper, chopped
 1 tablespoon chopped fresh basil
 1¼ cups beef broth
 2 tablespoons olive oil
 3 tablespoons lemon juice
 1 large avocado, cubed

Stir to blend. Chill.

Serves 4–6

To serve, pour soup into chilled bowls and top each with two slices of cucumber, a dollop of sour cream, a snip of dill.

GAZPACHO II

3 pieces French bread
4 very ripe tomatoes, peeled and
   chopped
1 cucumber, chopped
3 tablespoons olive oil
2 cups water
2 cups beef consommé
3 cloves garlic, peeled
2 tablespoons red wine vinegar
1 teaspoon ground cumin
1 tablespoon fresh sweet basil
2 teaspoons salt

Combine and let sit one hour. Then purée in blender and chill.

1 green pepper, minced
1 large tomato, peeled, seeded and
   diced
1 cucumber, minced
1 cup croutons

Serve gazpacho very cold with condiments in separate bowls for self-service.

Serves 4

STUFFED TOMATO SALADS

6 large tomatoes

For each tomato, cut off stem end, peel, and cut into 6 wedges almost to the base. Spread open and stuff with filling.

Chicken Filling

- **2 cups diced cooked chicken**
- **³/₄ cup diced celery**
- **2 tablespoons minced green onions**
- **7-ounce can mandarin oranges, drained**
- **1 teaspoon lemon juice**
- **¹/₂ cup mayonnaise**
- **¹/₄ cup chutney**

Mix and chill.

Curried Tuna Filling

- **Three 6-ounce cans tuna, drained**
- **¹/₂ cup diced celery**
- **1 tart apple, diced**
- **¹/₂ cup grapes, cut in half**
- **2 teaspoons grated onion**
- **2 teaspoons curry powder**
- **1 cup mayonnaise**
- **¹/₃ cup almonds, toasted and slivered**

Mix and chill.

Guacamole Filling

2 ripe avocados, mashed
1 teaspoon lemon juice
1 teaspoon salt
$^1/_2$ teaspoon Tabasco
2 tablespoons grated onion
1 tomato, peeled, drained, and diced

Mix and chill.

Serves 6

TOMATO SALAD VINAIGRETTE

4–6 tomatoes, peeled and cut into sixths
Fresh butter lettuce

Arrange on individual plates and chill.

2 egg yolks, beaten
1 clove garlic
1 teaspoon dry mustard
Dash of ground pepper

Mix in a blender.

$^1/_2$ cup olive oil

Drizzle in with blender on high.

Juice of $^1/_2$ lemon
1 tablespoon chopped fresh basil
3 tablespoons vinegar
$^1/_3$ cup sour cream (optional)

Slowly add. Chill, then pour over tomatoes.

Serves 4–6

MARINATED TOMATOES

10–12 tomatoes, peeled and sliced
  1 red onion, thinly sliced

Combine in a bowl.

  1 **cup olive oil**
$^1/_3$ **cup wine vinegar**
  2 **teaspoons oregano or**
    1 tablespoon minced fresh basil
  1 **teaspoon salt**
$^1/_2$ **teaspoon dry mustard**
$^1/_2$ **teaspoon freshly ground pepper**
  2 **cloves garlic, minced**

Combine and mix well. Pour over tomatoes and onions. Cover and refrigerate 2 to 4 hours, basting occasionally.

Serves 8–10

Sprinkle with parsley to serve.

MARINATED MUSHROOMS, TOMATOES, AND ARTICHOKE HEARTS

½ pound whole mushrooms
1 jar marinated artichoke hearts, undrained
¼ cup olive oil
5 tablespoons wine vinegar
¼ teaspoon dried basil
¼ teaspoon dried oregano
½ teaspoon dry mustard
1 small clove garlic, chopped
½ teaspoon salt
Dash of pepper

Combine and put in plastic bag. Seal. Chill 4 hours or overnight.

2 cups cherry tomatoes

Pour boiling water over tomatoes, then quickly skin. Add to marinade 3 hours before serving.

Serves 4

TOMATOES STUFFED WITH CHARD AND PINE NUTS

  2 **tablespoons olive oil**
  ½ **cup pine nuts**

Sauté until light brown.

  2 **tablespoons olive oil**
  1 **large onion, chopped**
  2 **cloves garlic, mashed**

Add and sauté until soft. Remove from heat.

  1 **cup cooked chopped, drained chard**
     (or spinach)
  2 **tablespoons olive oil**

Add and mix.

  6 **medium tomatoes**
     Salt and pepper
1–2 **teaspoons sugar**
  2 **tablespoons minced fresh basil**

Hollow cavities of tomatoes. Sprinkle insides with seasonings. Stuff with chard mixture.

  2 **tablespoons olive oil**

Arrange tomatoes in baking pan. Drizzle olive oil over. Bake at 350° for 15 minutes. Chill, then bring to room temperature before serving.

Serves 6

FRIED RIPE TOMATOES

Tomatoes
Salt and pepper
Cracker crumbs
Butter

Slice tomatoes 1 inch thick. Season. Dip in egg, then cracker crumbs. Dry 1 hour in refrigerator. Fry in butter. Drain.

SAUTÉED CHERRY TOMATOES

½ **cup butter**
2 **green onions, minced**
½ **clove garlic, minced**
1 **tablespoon minced fresh basil**
    (or 2 teaspoons dried)
1 **tablespoon minced fresh parsley**

Heat over high flame, stirring.

2 **dozen cherry tomatoes**

Add to pan, shaking pan until skins begin to wrinkle. Remove from heat and serve.

Serves 4–6

HERBED TOMATOES

6 **whole tomatoes, peeled
    with stems on**
²/₃ **cup olive oil**
¹/₄ **cup wine vinegar**
¹/₄ **cup minced fresh parsley**
1 **clove garlic, minced**
¹/₄ **cup minced green onion**
1 **tablespoon minced fresh basil**
1 **teaspoon minced fresh dill**
1 **teaspoon salt**
   Freshly ground pepper to taste.

Marinate several hours, basting occasionally.

Serves 6

Spectacular in a big glass bowl for a buffet. Peeled cherry tomatoes are great as well. For simpler functions use the same dressing on sliced tomatoes.

TABBOULEH

2 cups fine bulghur or cracked wheat

Cover with warm water. Let stand until fluffy. Drain well, squeezing out extra water.

1½ cups seeded, chopped tomatoes
1 cup minced fresh parsley
½ cup minced fresh mint
½ cup minced scallions

Add to wheat and stir.

½ cup lemon juice
½ cup olive oil
2 teaspoons salt
Pepper to taste

Add and stir. Chill to blend flavors.

Serves 6

This unusual salad from the Middle East is a good accompaniment to barbecued meat.

ANCHOVY STUFFED
BAKED TOMATOES

  6 **large tomatoes**
     Salt and pepper

Cut off tops and scoop out pulp, leaving shell ½ inch thick. Season, then turn upside down to drain.

  3 **tablespoons olive oil**
  2 **cloves garlic, minced**
  3 **green onions, minced**

Sauté and remove from heat.

   2 **cups cooked rice**
  ¼ **cup fresh parsley, minced**
8–10 **anchovies, minced**
   1 **teaspoon minced fresh mint**
  ¼ **teaspoon pepper**

Add to onions and mix well. Stuff tomatoes. Place in buttered casserole and bake at 350° for 15 minutes to heat.

Serves 6

TOMATOES PROVENÇAL

2 tablespoons olive oil
2 tablespoons lemon juice
4 large tomatoes, peeled,
    halved, juiced, and seeded
  Salt and freshly ground pepper

Place tomatoes cut side up in buttered casserole and drizzle oil and juice over. Season. Bake 5 minutes at 450°.

½ cup fresh bread crumbs
1–2 cloves garlic, minced
1 teaspoon minced fresh basil
¼ cup minced fresh parsley
2 tablespoons minced shallots or
    green onions

Sprinkle over tomatoes. Return to oven for 3 minutes to brown crumbs.

Serves 4–6

FRIED GREEN TOMATOES

Green tomatoes
Sugar
Flour
Butter

Slice ½ inch thick. Sprinkle lightly with sugar. Dredge with flour. Let dry in refrigerator for 20 minutes. Fry in butter. Drain.

Some aficionados grow tomatoes just to have the green ones. Delicious with bacon for breakfast.

CURRIED GREEN TOMATOES

2 **large green tomatoes, sliced**
1 **small onion, sliced**
1 **teaspoon curry powder**
Salt and pepper to taste
3 **tablespoons butter**

Sauté onion in butter. Add curry. Add tomatoes, and fry until cooked. Season and serve.

Serves 2

FRIED EGG AND TOMATO SUPPER, SICILIAN STYLE

    2 thick 1½-inch slices tomato
    1 tablespoon butter
    2 slices garlic

Sauté.

    2 eggs
    1 tablespoon butter

Sauté eggs in separate pan.

    1   tablespoon butter
    1–2 sliced garlic cloves
         Chopped fresh basil
         Chopped fresh parsley

Sauté garlic. Put egg on tomato and pour garlic butter over. Sprinkle with basil and parsley.

Serves 1

SPANISH RICE

1½ **cups peeled, seeded, quartered tomatoes**
2 **teaspoons salt**

Purée in blender.

2 **onions, chopped**
3 **cloves garlic, minced**
¼ **cup oil**

Sauté until soft in large skillet.

2 **cups uncooked rice**

Add and sauté. Stir in tomatoes.

3 **cups boiling water**

Add and simmer, covered, over low heat 20 to 25 minutes.

Serves 8

For curried rice, add ½ teaspoon ground ginger and ¼ teaspoon each ground cloves, coriander and pepper to the onions and garlic and sauté for 2 minutes more.

FRESH TOMATO BAKE

**8 medium tomatoes, peeled
and quartered
1 teaspoon salt
$^1/_8$ teaspoon pepper
1 teaspoon sugar
$^1/_2$ teaspoon dry mustard**

Mix well.

**2 tablespoons butter
2 large onions, sliced**

Sauté 5 minutes.

**2$^1/_2$ cups fresh bread crumbs
6 tablespoons butter, melted**

Mix until blended. In a buttered 1$^1/_2$-quart casserole layer tomatoes, onions, then crumbs. Bake at 350° for 25 minutes.

$^1/_4$ cup grated Parmesan cheese

Sprinkle with cheese. Bake 5 minutes more.

Serves 6

Very easy, very good.

TOMATOES ON THE SHELL

1 large tomato, peeled

Cut into 4 slices and place on 4 scallop shells.

1 teaspoon olive oil
2 teaspoons lemon juice
2 teaspoons minced fresh parsley
1 teaspoon minced fresh dill
1 teaspoon chopped chives
Salt and freshly ground pepper
2 teaspoons grated cheese

Sprinkle each tomato slice in given order. Bake 6 minutes at 500°. Serve at once.

Serves 4

Vary the cheese according to the menu. Use cheddar for heavier meat dishes or barbecued steaks. Use mild, white cheese for poultry or seafood.

STACKED TOMATOES

4 tomatoes, peeled and halved
   Salt and pepper to taste
½ cup mayonnaise
½ cup minced green onion
1 cup grated cheddar cheese

Place tomatoes in buttered casserole and top with rest of ingredients in given order. Bake at 325° for 20 minutes.

Serves 4

TOMATO AND CHEESE STRATA

        2   teaspoons oil
        2   onions, minced
        2   cloves garlic, minced
      1–2   green peppers, minced

Sauté 5 minutes.

       12   medium tomatoes, peeled and sliced
        1   can tomato paste
            Dashes of cayenne, salt, pepper,
            dried parsley, oregano
        3   cans peeled and diced jalapeño
            peppers

Add and simmer 20 to 30 minutes until thickened.

       16   slices bread, buttered and cubed
       ½   pound cheddar cheese, grated

In a buttered 9-by-13 pan, layer half the bread, the tomato sauce, half the cheese, remaining bread, and cheese.

        6   eggs
        4   cups milk
        2   teaspoons dry mustard
        1   teaspoon salt
        1   teaspoon pepper

Mix and pour over casserole. Cover and refrigerate overnight or at least 6 hours. Bake at 350° for 50 to 60 minutes.

Serves 8

The perfect brunch dish.

FRESH TOMATO CAKE

- 1 cup dark brown sugar
- ½ cup shortening
- 2 eggs
- ½ cup chopped nuts
- ½ cup chopped dates
- ½ cup raisins
- 2 cups peeled, cubed tomatoes
- 3 cups sifted flour
- 2 teaspoons baking powder
- 1 teaspoon baking soda
- 1 teaspoon nutmeg
- ½ teaspoon salt

Cream sugar and shortening. Add eggs, nuts, dates, raisins, and tomatoes. Sift dry ingredients into tomato mixture. Pour into greased and floured 9-by-13-inch pan. Bake at 350° for 30 minutes.

- 8 ounces cream cheese
- 1½ cups confectioner's sugar
- 3 tablespoons butter
- 1 teaspoon vanilla
  Pinch of salt

Beat with electric mixer until smooth. Frost cooled cake.

Serves 8

A good spice cake with weird ingredients.

TOO MANY TOMATOES SAUCE

2 large onions, chopped
2 cloves garlic, minced
$^1/_3$ cup olive oil

Sauté until golden, about 10 minutes, in large pot.

15 large tomatoes

Peel, cut into eighths, and add to pot.

2 cups red wine
12 ounces tomato paste
$1^1/_2$ teaspoons salt
$^1/_4$ teaspoon pepper
2 heaping teaspoons dried oregano
1 teaspoon dried basil
1 teaspoon crushed dried rosemary

Add to pot, bring to boil, then simmer 1 hour uncovered.

5 pints

Very ripe tomatoes make the best sauce. Freeze in bags or containers if you like.

PIPERADE SAUCE

4 **green peppers, peeled, seeded,
   veined, and cut in thin strips**
1 **onion, minced**
2 **tablespoons olive oil**

Sauté 5 minutes.

4 **tomatoes, peeled, seeded, and
     chopped**
1 **clove garlic, minced**
½ **teaspoon salt
   Freshly ground pepper to taste**

Add and simmer about 5 minutes, until thickened.

1 **tablespoon butter**
6 **very thin slices smoked ham,
     cut in strips**

Sauté 5 minutes. Stir into tomato sauce.

Serves 4

*A traditional sauce from southern France. Serve over
omelets or just add to eggs and scramble.*

OLD-FASHIONED
TOMATO PUDDING

5 cups peeled sliced tomatoes

Place in large kettle.

9 whole cloves
6 whole peppercorns
$^1/_8$ teaspoon dried basil
1 bay leaf
$^1/_2$ teaspoon salt
$^1/_8$ teaspoon dried tarragon

Put together in 6-inch square of cheesecloth. Tie with string. Add to tomatoes. Simmer 30 minutes, stirring occasionally. Remove bag.

3 slices bread, diced
$^3/_4$ cup brown sugar
1 teaspoon minced green onions
2 teaspoons butter

Stir into tomatoes. Pour into buttered 2-quart casserole. Bake at 400° for 45 to 55 minutes.

Serves 6

TOMATO PIE

1 cup biscuit mix
¼ cup water
1 tablespoon soft butter

Mix with fork and press into a 9-inch pie pan.

**4–5 medium tomatoes, peeled and
sliced ½ inch thick**

Layer slices on crust.

1 cup shredded cheddar cheese

Sprinkle atop.

½ cup mayonnaise
1–2 green onions, minced
2 tablespoons minced fresh parsley

Mix and spread over cheese. Bake at 350° for 30 minutes in lower half of oven. Serve immediately.

Serves 6

A good accompaniment to barbecued hamburgers for summer fare.

SAUTÉED BEEF WITH TOMATOES AND PEPPERS

$1/_2$ **pound fresh mushrooms, sliced**
1 **large garlic clove, mashed**
5 **green onions, cut in**
  1-inch pieces
4 **tablespoons butter**

Sauté in large skillet. Remove and set aside.

2 **pounds top sirloin, cut in**
  $1/_2$**-by-**$1/_2$**-by-2-inch slices**
$1/_3$ **cup flour**
2 **tablespoons oil**

Coat meat in flour. Sauté, a few pieces at a time, in same skillet 3 minutes.

$1/_2$ **teaspoon pepper**
2 **teaspoons paprika**
1 **teaspoon dried basil**
1 **teaspoon dried oregano**
  Dash of nutmeg

Combine and sprinkle over meat.

$1/_4$ **cup lemon juice**
$1/_2$ **cup red wine**
1 **beef bouillon cube**

Add to skillet, and stir to dissolve bouillon cube.

1 **green pepper, cut in strips**
12 **cherry tomatoes, halved**

Add to skillet. Stir in mushroom mixture. Cover and cook 10 minutes.

¹/₄ cup brandy, heated

Add and flame.

Serves 6

Serve over noodles or rice with salad, French bread, and red wine.

TOMATO SALSA

  4 **medium tomatoes, peeled and
     minced**
  ½ **cup minced onion**
  ½ **cup minced celery**
  ¼ **cup minced green pepper**
  2 **tablespoons wine vinegar**
  3 **tablespoons olive oil**
  1 **teaspoon salt**
  1 **tablespoon sugar**
  ½ **teaspoon dried basil or rosemary**
1–2 **canned green chilis, minced**

Combine and blend well. Cover and chill several hours or overnight.

2 cups

Serve as an appetizer with corn or tortilla chips; as a first course salad piled into halves of avocados; as a relish for grilled fish, meats, or Mexican food.

FRESH TOMATO CATSUP

16 cups tomatoes, peeled, sliced
3 white onions, sliced
1 cup vinegar
1 glove garlic, sliced
½ cup brown sugar
1½ teaspoons ground mace
1½ teaspoons pepper
1½ teaspoons ground cloves
1½ teaspoons celery salt
1 tablespoon salt
2 dashes of Tabasco

Simmer uncovered until thick, about 3 hours. Stir frequently to mash tomatoes and to prevent burning. Purée in blender. Pour into sterilized jars and seal.

9 pints

CHILI SAUCE

10 large tomatoes, peeled and
      quartered
 2 onions, minced
 2 red or green peppers, minced
½ cup sugar
 1 tablespoon salt
1½ cups cider vinegar
 1 teaspoon ground cloves
 1 teaspoon cinnamon
 1 teaspoon allspice
 1 teaspoon Tabasco (add more
      to taste when cooked)

Mix in heavy kettle. Simmer over very low heat about 2 hours, until quite thick.

2½ pints

A nice gift from the garden for Christmas.

TOO MANY TOMATOES RELISH

8 cups ripe tomatoes, chopped
1 cup celery, chopped
1 large onion, chopped
1 cup green peppers, chopped

Combine in a colander and drain for one hour.

1 cup cider vinegar
1 cup honey
2 teaspoons paprika
2 tablespoons salt
1 tablespoon mustard seed
1 tablespoon pickling spices

Combine in a saucepan and bring to a boil for 5 minutes. Cool and then pour over vegetables. Let stand overnight. Pack in cold, sterile jars. Cover, but do not seal. Refrigerates up to three months.

6 pints

A peak-of-the-season treatment for ripe tomatoes.

TOMATO CHUTNEY

12 ripe peeled tomatoes
 4 onions
 2 large sweet peppers
 6 tart peeled apples

Chop and combine in a large kettle.

3 cups brown sugar
3 cups cider vinegar
1 cup raisins
1 tablespoon powdered ginger
2 teaspoons salt
1 teaspoon chili powder
1 teaspoon cinnamon
1 clove garlic, minced

Add, bring to a boil, and then simmer until thick. Cook slowly to prevent scorching. Pour into hot sterilized jars and seal.

8 pints

GREEN TOMATO PICKLES

25 large green tomatoes

Wash, core, and slice the tomatoes about $1/3$-inch thick and pack into five hot sterilized quart jars.

10 tablespoons dill seed
10 peeled garlic cloves
5 whole cloves
2 tablespoons pickling spices
$2^1/_2$ teaspoons cayenne pepper

Divide equally among the jars.

4 cups vinegar
4 cups water
$1/_3$ cup salt

Heat to boiling and then pour over tomatoes to within $1/_4$-inch of the jar top. Seal and process twenty minutes in boiling water. Let stand four weeks to season.

5 quarts

GREEN TOMATO CHOW-CHOW

- 16 cups green tomatoes
- 1 large head cabbage
- 8 onions
- 6 green peppers
- 6 sweet red peppers
- ½ cup salt

Chop and combine all vegetables in a large kettle. Stir in salt and let stand at room temperature overnight. Drain.

- 15 cups vinegar
- 5 cups sugar
- 3 tablespoons dry mustard
- 1 tablespoon powdered ginger
- 1 tablespoon turmeric

Combine in a large kettle.

- 4 tablespoons mustard seed
- 3 tablespoons celery seed
- 2 tablespoons pickling spices

Put together in a 6-inch square of cheese-cloth. Tie with a string and add to the kettle. Bring the liquid to a boil and then simmer 30 minutes. Add vegetables and return to simmer for 30 minutes. Discard spice bag. Spoon into hot sterilized jars and seal.

16–18 pints

TURNIPS

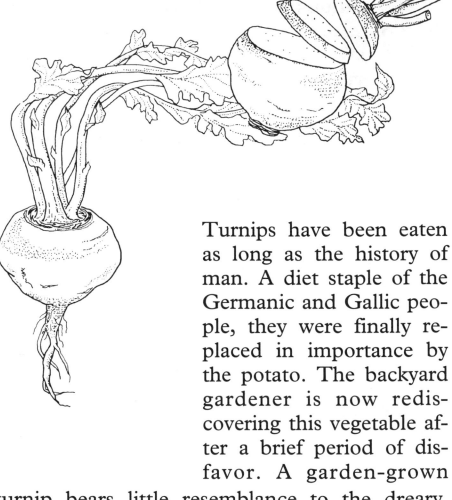

Turnips have been eaten as long as the history of man. A diet staple of the Germanic and Gallic people, they were finally replaced in importance by the potato. The backyard gardener is now rediscovering this vegetable after a brief period of disfavor. A garden-grown turnip bears little resemblance to the dreary, aging globe labeled turnip at the local grocery store. Commercial turnips are too big, too pithy, too old, and otherwise undesirable. A turnip freshly plucked from the ground, raw and thinly sliced, has a delicate flavor somewhere between that of an apple and a radish. The turnip is a very-cool season crop, stores well, and requires little care, so it is a good early spring or fall choice.

Turnips are considered a root crop, although the tender young greens are also edible, and are much higher in vitamin content. The leaves on older plants get coarse and bitter. Even the young leaves can be too sharp; mix in some lettuce leaves to soften the taste. Use the turnip thinnings for very tender greens. There are a few turnip varieties developed just for the greens.

(Rutabagas, a near relative, are frequently lumped into the turnip category. Their flavor is less delicate and cultivation much longer, so they are not a likely choice for most climates and tastes.)

The Growing Turnips require 35 to 60 days to mature from seed, depending on the variety. They are hardy to cold and can take temperatures just below freezing. They don't like it much hotter than 85°. Plant them in early spring or late summer. Pick the variety which will mature in time with the local weather pattern. Plant seeds ½ inch deep, in rows spaced 1–2 feet apart. Thin to stand 3–4 inches apart. Plant a couple of crops each season to avoid too many turnips at once. Although the turnip, like all root plants, likes light soil, it is not very temperamental. A relative of the cabbage, it is susceptible to the same diseases, so it should not be planted in the same spot as any of its relatives.

The Harvest A turnip should be about 2 inches across when harvested, and it should be moist and crisp. Harvest by pulling at the base of the leaves. Use the greens immediately, or discard.

The Basics
1 pound = 4 two-inch turnips = 2 cups sliced = 3 servings.
$2/_3$ cup cooked turnip (3.5 ounces) = 23 calories, 4.9 grams carbohydrates, .8 grams protein, more than half recommended daily vitamin C.
$2/_3$ cup cooked turnip greens (3.5 ounces) = 20 calories, 3.6 grams carbohydrates, 2.2 grams protein, very high in vitamins C and A.
10-foot row = about 40 turnips.

The Storage Cut off greens and store turnips in a bag in a cool, damp place or in the crisper drawer of the refrigerator. They will last nicely about 2 weeks, sometimes longer.

Freezing Peel and dice or slice. Scald $2^1/_2$ to 3 minutes. Chill in cold water, drain, and package in bags of convenient size. Freeze. Frozen turnips are good in casseroles or stews, but they lose some of their crispness and are not suitable for simple preparation.

The Cooking Always peel turnips. The skins are quite bitter. Turnips may be cooked whole, diced, sliced, grated, or even cut into small balls with a melon baller. *Steamed turnips:* Steam whole turnips 20 to 30 minutes. Mash or slice and serve with butter and salt.

Complementary Herbs Celery seeds, bay leaves, allspice.

TURNIP GREENS

4   slices bacon
1   onion, chopped

Fry bacon in large skillet. Crumble. Sauté onion in bacon grease.

6   cups chopped turnip greens

Add greens to skillet. Cover and cook over low heat 5 to 7 minutes.

Salt and pepper to taste

Add crumbled bacon, season and serve.

Serves 4

Serve the greens Southern style with fresh, sweet corn bread and butter.

SCALLOPED TURNIPS
AND ONIONS

2 **cups thinly sliced turnips**
1 **cup thinly sliced onions**
5 **tablespoons butter**
3 **tablespoons flour**
  Salt

Layer, dotting each layer with butter and sprinkling with flour and salt.

1¼ **cups beef consommé**

Pour over and bake 1½ hours at 350°.

Serves 4

TURNIPS WITH A DIP

2 cups sour cream
8 ounces cream cheese
1 tablespoon grated onion
¼ teaspoon Worcestershire sauce
3 ounces chipped beef, shredded

Mix. Let stand 1 hour.

Raw turnips have a fresh crunchy texture that is lost in cooking. Many find turnips served this way most pleasing (particularly if they don't know in advance what they're eating). Peel and cut turnips in wedges. Serve around a bowl of dip topped with minced parsley.

LAMB VEGETABLE STEW

1½ cups chopped onion
 3 large carrots, diced thinly
 8 cups hot water
 1 tablespoon salt
    Leg of lamb bone and/or
      1-1½ pounds lamb neck
 1 cup diced turnips
½ cup pearl barley

Mix in large saucepan. Simmer covered 3 hours.

 1 cup peas

Add, cook 10 minutes more.

Serves 8–10

Excellent reheated.

TURNIP AND CARROT SLAW

  4 cups grated turnips
  2 cups grated carrots
  1 Bermuda onion, chopped

Toss in bowl.

  ¾ cup sugar
  1 cup cider vinegar
  ½ cup oil
  1 teaspoon celery seed
  1 teaspoon dry mustard
  1 teaspoon salt

Bring to a boil. Pour over vegetables. Chill.

Serves 6–8

MASHED TURNIPS

**6–8 small young turnips, peeled and
sliced
3 slices bacon**

Boil uncovered about 30 minutes. Discard bacon
and drain turnips.

**2 tablespoons butter
Salt and pepper to taste
Dashes of cayenne pepper (optional)**

Purée turnips, adding butter and seasonings.

Serves 6

TURNIP SOUFFLÉ

  6 **turnips, cooked and mashed**
  2 **egg yolks, beaten**
  2 **tablespoons butter, melted**
  ½ **cup milk**
  ¼ **cup grated mild cheese**
     Salt and pepper to taste
     Dash of cayenne pepper

Mix well.

  3 **egg whites, beaten**

Fold in. Place in buttered soufflé dish. Bake 30 minutes at 325°.

Serves 4–6

Much to everyone's surprise, this is elegant and delicious. Serve with roast beef and a green vegetable.

TURNIP RING

1 onion, chopped
2 tablespoons butter

Sauté until soft.

1 cup mashed turnips
¾ cup mashed potatoes
1 cup crushed butter crackers
2 eggs, beaten
¼ cup light cream
   Salt and pepper to taste
   Dash of cayenne pepper

Add and mix well. Pour into greased ring mold.
Bake 1 hour at 350°.

Serves 6

IRISH LAMB STEW

2–3 **pounds boneless lamb, cubed**
¼ **cup flour**
1 **teaspoon salt**
1 **teaspoon dry mustard**

Shake flour, salt, and mustard onto meat to coat.

2 **tablespoons oil**

Sauté meat in Dutch oven until browned.

2 **large onions, quartered**
1 **small carrot, diced**
2 **stalks celery, sliced**
3 **turnips, quartered**
¼ **teaspoon dried marjoram**
¼ **teaspoon dried thyme**
¼ **teaspoon salt**
2 **cups water**

Add, cover, and simmer 1½ hours.

1 **cup fresh peas**
2 **tablespoons sugar**
2 **tablespoons cider vinegar**
2 **tablespoons flour**
2 **tablespoons water**
1 **teaspoon dry mustard**

Mix, then stir into stew. Simmer 10 minutes.

Serves 6

STIR-FRIED TURNIPS WITH HAM

   8 **turnips**
   4 **tablespoons vegetable oil**

Peel turnips. Grate. Sauté 1 minute, stirring constantly.

   1 **cup beef broth**
  ½ **teaspoon salt**
      Freshly ground pepper to taste

Add. Bring to a boil. Cover and cook over low heat 5 minutes.

  ¼ **cup thinly sliced green onions**
   1 **tablespoon soy sauce**
 1½ **cups thinly sliced ham**

Add. Simmer uncovered 3 minutes.

Serves 4–6

Serve this Chinese dish with steamed rice.

ANYTHING AND EVERYTHING

This chapter is for those gardeners who feel a bit like Jack, whose beanstalk grew to heaven overnight. Even the wisest garden planner and expert kitchen techniques cannot prevent the inevitable deluge of fresh produce. Usually, this is an August occurrence, and tomatoes and summer squash are the frequent culprits. But an overzealous planting of broccoli or spring vegetables can cause the problem any time of the year. The refrigerator is loaded with fresh vegetables, and it seems pure frustration to pick one over the other.

The recipes in this chapter utilize an assortment of vegetables and are special in their flexibility for substitution. One of the most beautiful of all vegetable presentations is the seasonal platter. Arrange a large serving tray with lettuce. Make separate piles of the vegetables in season. Some may be marinated, some cooked, and some raw. Arrange for color. The trick to all vegetable cooking is to experiment. Use the largest quantities of whatever seems to be overtaking the garden.

Also included are some general suggestions for butters and sauces. The butters, in particular, are an excellent means of complementing the fresh taste of garden produce, varying the presentation and avoiding long hours in the kitchen.

ASSORTED BUTTERS

These butters may be mixed and matched to any vegetable choice. A good rule of thumb is to remember to use 1 tablespoon butter for every cup of cooked vegetables.

½ cup butter, creamed

Butter must always be creamed before seasoning is added.

Lemon Butter

Beat in 1½ tablespoons lemon juice, 2 teaspoons fresh minced parsley, ½ teaspoon salt. Cover and refrigerate to blend flavors.

Mustard Butter

Beat in 1–2 tablespoons Dijon mustard and ¼ teaspoon salt. Cover and chill. Excellent with asparagus or cauliflower.

Soy Butter

Beat in 1 tablespoon lemon juice and 2 tablespoons soy sauce. Cover and chill. Best with tender-crisp cabbage or snow peas.

Anchovy Butter

Beat in 2 teaspoons anchovy paste, 2 teaspoons lemon juice, and 1 tablespoon favorite herb. Cover and chill.

Garlic Butter

Beat in 3–4 mashed garlic cloves, ¼ teaspoon salt, and 2–4 tablespoons fresh minced parsley. Parboil garlic for milder flavor.

Green Onion Butter

Heat 2 minced green onions, ¼ cup red wine, and ¼ cup beef broth until liquid is reduced to a few tablespoons. Let cool and then beat into butter. Cover and chill.

Herb Butter

Beat in 1 tablespoon lemon juice and 2 table-spoons minced fresh mixed herbs: tarragon, basil, or parsley. Try to keep some of this butter in your refrigerator at all times.

Hot Lemon Butter

Add 2 tablespoons lemon juice and ½ teaspoon Worcestershire sauce to butter. Heat until melted and serve.

HOLLANDAISE

3 **egg yolks**
2 **tablespoons lemon juice**
¼ **teaspoon salt**
   Pinch of cayenne pepper

Purée in blender at low speed.

½ **cup butter**

Heat in a small saucepan until bubbly. With blender running, drizzle butter slowly into egg mixture. Serve immediately or reheat by placing in a pan of hot water.

1 cup

This is a foolproof hollandaise. Butter should be very hot. Margarine will not work.

WHITE SAUCE

3 tablespoons butter
3 tablespoons flour

Make a roux by melting butter, stirring in flour, and cooking slowly, stirring, about 2 minutes.

2 cups heated milk or stock

Add all the milk or stock at once. Stir over high heat until sauce begins to bubble. Using a wire whisk ensures a smooth sauce.

VARIATIONS

Curry Sauce

Add ½ cup minced onions to roux. After milk is added, stir in 2–3 teaspoons curry powder blended with a few tablespoons of the cream sauce and stir to blend.

Sauce Suprême

Add ¼ cup heavy cream and 1 beaten egg yolk to white sauce. Stir in 2 diced hard-boiled eggs and serve. Best on spinach, broccoli, and asparagus.

Mornay Sauce

Add ¹/₂ cup grated Swiss cheese and 2 tablespoons vermouth to sauce.

Velouté Sauce

Add ¹/₃ cup peeled, chopped, drained tomatoes; 1–2 tablespoons minced fresh basil is a nice addition too.

Cheddar Cheese Sauce

Stir in 2 cups grated cheddar cheese until cheese melts. Pour over vegetables and sprinkle with paprika.

2 cups

HOMEMADE MAYONNAISE

 2 **tablespoons lemon juice**
 1 **egg**
 ½ **teaspoon salt**
 ½ **teaspoon dry mustard**
 ¼ **cup salad oil**

Purée in blender.

 ¾ **cup olive oil**

With blender running, drizzle slowly into mixture until thickened.

1¼ cups

VARIATIONS

Watercress Mayonnaise

Add ½ cup sour cream, dashes of tarragon and salt, and ¼ cup minced watercress.

Sauce Rémoulade

Add 2 minced anchovies, 2 minced green onions, 1 tablespoon chopped dill pickle and 1 tablespoon minced parsley.

Aïoli Sauce

Add 4 mashed cloves garlic.

Mayonnaise Verte

Add ¼ cup minced herbs, such as chives, spinach or parsley.

ANTIPASTO

²/₃ **cup olive oil**
¹/₃ **cup wine vinegar**
2 **tablespoons minced celery**
2 **cloves garlic, halved**
¹/₄ **cup minced fresh parsley**
¹/₄ **teaspoon salt**
¹/₈ **teaspoon dried oregano**

Combine in a jar. Cover and let stand. Shake before using.

> **Tomatoes, thickly sliced**
> **Sweet red and green peppers, sliced**
> **Large prawns, cooked and peeled**
> **Cauliflower, parboiled and cut into**
>   **flowerets**

Place in separate bowls. Pour marinade over each and let sit 2 to 6 hours.

> **Salami, sliced**
> **Smoked salmon, sliced**
> **Cheeses, sliced**
> **Anchovies**
> **Tuna, drained**

Arrange with marinated ingredients on a large platter.

Serves 6–12

Serve with sourdough bread to soak up the juices.

460

BAGNA CAUDA

¼ cup olive oil
¼ cup butter
4 small cloves garlic, mashed
2 ounces anchovies, drained and chopped
3 tablespoons minced fresh parsley

Combine and heat until bubbly. Serve in a chafing dish, keeping hot.

Red cabbage, cut into small wedges
Cauliflower, cut into flowerets
Cherry tomatoes
Green beans, cut in 1-inch pieces
Sweet green and red peppers, cubed
Mushroom caps
Radishes
Turnips, sliced thickly
Summer squash, cut in ½-inch pieces

Arrange any combination on a platter with bamboo cocktail skewers.

French bread, thinly sliced

To serve, each guest skewers vegetable and swirls it in the hot dip. Place atop bread and eat.

Serves 8

Bagna Cauda is Italian for "hot bath." Everybody cooks his own and makes a hot vegetable sandwich. Fun and good.

COLD GARDEN SOUP

6 ripe tomatoes, peeled and chopped
½ cup minced green peppers
¼ cup minced green onions
½ cup minced celery
½ cup minced cucumbers
½ cup minced carrots
1½ cups tomato juice
1½ cups beef broth
2 tablespoons vinegar
2 tablespoons olive oil
1 teaspoon salt
½ teaspoon dried dill weed
Dash of chili powder
Dash of pepper
Dash of garlic salt

Combine, cover, and chill at least 4 hours.

Serves 6

MINESTRONE

¼ **medium cabbage, shredded**
1 **leek, chopped**
6–12 **leaves chard, chopped**
6 **stalks celery, chopped**
4 **cups water**

Combine in large kettle. Simmer 20 minutes.

2 **slices bacon**

Fry and remove from skillet. Use bacon for another purpose.

1 **onion, chopped**
1 **clove garlic, minced**

Sauté in bacon grease 5 minutes.

1 **cup tomato purée**
2 **cups tomatoes, peeled, seeded**

Add to onions, stir and cook for a few minutes. Then add all to cabbage mixture.

5 **ounces dried lima beans, cooked**
   and mashed
2–3 **teaspoons salt**
2–3 **teaspoons chopped fresh basil**
1 **teaspoon pepper**

Add to soup and cook 1 hour more.

5 **ounces split peas, cooked**
   Summer squash, cubed

Eggplant, parboiled and cubed
5 **ounces dried kidney beans, cooked**
3 **ounces macaroni, cooked**

Add and simmer 20 to 30 minutes. Serve warm.

Serves 8–10

A masterpiece! Serve with freshly grated Parmesan cheese, a green salad, and Chianti.

WEIGHT WATCHERS' SOUP

3 **zucchini, diced**
3 **stalks celery, diced**
¼ **pound mushrooms, diced**
½ **medium cabbage, diced**
4 **tomatoes, peeled and diced**
4 **cups tomato juice**
3 **cups beef broth**
2 **tablespoons grated onion**
1 **teaspoon dried Italian seasonmg**
½ **clove garlic, chopped**
Salt and pepper to taste

Mix all together ill a large kettle. Simmer 45 minutes. Serve warm or chilled.

Serves 8

Stores well for at least a week.

QUICHE PASTRY SHELL

6   tablespoons butter
2   tablespoons lard or vegetable
      shortening
1½   cups flour
¼   teaspoon salt
3   tablespoons cold water

Cut butter and shortening into dry ingredients. Stir in enough water to hold dough together. Chill 1 hour. Roll out and place in a tart or quiche pan. Prick all over with a fork, cover with foil, and fill with dried beans to weight crust down. Bake 8 minutes at 450 degrees. Remove beans and foil, prick again, and bake 10 minutes more.

DELICATESSEN
MARINATED VEGETABLES

$^1/_2$ head cauliflower
2 carrots
2 celery stalks
2 red or green sweet peppers
$^1/_2$ cup snap beans

Cut all into bite-sized pieces.

$^2/_3$ cup vinegar
$^1/_2$ cup olive oil
1 tablespoon sugar
1 teaspoon salt
$^1/_2$ teaspoon dried basil
$^1/_2$ teaspoon dried tarragon
$^1/_4$ cup water

Pour over vegetables and bring to a boil. Cover and simmer 5 minutes. Cool and chill.

2 cups

VEGETABLE SALAD

  1–2 cups cooked vegetables
    1 head lettuce, torn
    2 carrots, sliced thinly
    2 stalks celery, sliced
    2 green onions, sliced
    1 avocado, sliced
  $1/3$ cup cottage cheese
    6 tablespoons olive oil

Mix in salad bowl.

    2 tablespoons red wine vinegar
    1 teaspoon Worcestershire sauce
  $1/4$ cup grated Parmesan cheese
    1 clove minced garlic
      Salt and pepper to taste

Add and toss.

Serves 4–6

Use whatever is available for the cooked vegetables.

MOLDED GARDEN SALAD

6-ounce package lemon gelatin
2 cups boiling water

Combine and stir to dissolve.

1¹/₃ cups cold water
¹/₃ cup lemon juice

Add and chill about 1 hour, until very thick.

1 small zucchini, chopped
¹/₂ cup diced cucumber
¹/₂ cup diced carrots
¹/₂ cup diced green onion

Fold into gelatin and pour into an oiled 1¹/₂-quart mold. Chill until firm, then unmold.

Serves 6–8

Garnish with crisp little radishes.

SALMON RELISH

4 medium tomatoes, chopped
2 green peppers, chopped
½ cup minced green onions
½ cup minced red onion
6 tablespoons minced canned green
  chilis
2 teaspoons salt

Mix together well, cover, and chill overnight.

2 cups

A delightful variation from hollandaise.

MIXED VEGETABLE STIR-FRY

Vegetable oil
Small zucchini, diagonally sliced
Celery, sliced
Sweet green or red peppers, sliced
Garlic, minced
Fresh ginger, sliced (use sparingly)

Heat oil over high flame in a wok or large pan. Add any combination of vegetables and stir until they are crisply cooked. Remove from heat.

1 **tablespoon cornstarch mixed with**
      2 tablespoons water
1 **tablespoon soy sauce**
      Tomatoes, peeled, seeded, and sliced

Stir into vegetables. Cover and simmer a few minutes.

Minced fresh parsley
Almonds, toasted and slivered
      (optional)

Sprinkle atop vegetables.

RAINBOW VEGETABLE RING

1   cup cooked spinach
1   cup cooked peas
1   tablespoon butter
2   tablespoons white sauce (page 456)
1   egg
    Pinches of salt and pepper
    Pinch of nutmeg

Purée in a blender. Pour into a buttered 1½-quart ring mold.

4   large carrots, cooked
1   tablespoon butter
1   tablespoon white sauce
1   tablespoon brown sugar
1   egg
    Pinch of cayenne pepper
    Pinch of salt

Purée in blender. Pour over first layer in mold.

1   large cauliflower, cooked
2   tablespoons grated white cheese
1   tablespoon butter
1   tablespoon white sauce
1   egg
    Pinch of dried basil
    Pinch of allspice

Purée and pour over carrot layer. Place the mold in a pan of hot water. Bake at 350° for 30 to 40 minutes. Unmold and serve.

Serves 8

Lovely to look at, a wonderful blend of flavors. The white sauce and egg in each layer bind the mold, but allow the flavor of the vegetables to dominate.

HOT POT

Raw prawns, peeled
Raw scallops
Tofu, cubed
Cabbage, sliced
Summer squash, cubed
Cauliflower, cut into flowerets
Asparagus, diagonally sliced
Snow peas
Green onions, diagonally sliced

Arrange attractively on platters.

Dry mustard mixed with water and
   soy sauce
Soy sauce
Plum sauce
Hoisin sauce
Oyster sauce

Place in separate bowls.

8 cups chicken broth

Heat to boiling in a chafing dish.

Hot cooked rice

Fill one bowl for each person.

Serves 4

Provide chopsticks for this Japanese meal. When all the ingredients are ready, drop a combination of vegetables and seafood into the hot broth. Each person picks out the cooked foods, dips them in chosen sauce, and eats with rice.

SHISH KEBOBS

½ cup lemon juice
¼ cup olive oil
3 green onions, minced
1 teaspoon ground ginger
1 teaspoon ground coriander
1 clove garlic, minced
2 teaspoons curry powder
2 teaspoons salt

Combine.

2 pounds lamb, cut into cubes

Add to marinade, and let sit, unrefrigerated, 2 to 8 hours. Drain, reserving marinade.

2 zucchini, cut in 1-inch pieces
2 green peppers, cubed
2 ears of corn, cut in 1-inch pieces
8 small boiling onions, peeled

Skewer, alternating vegetables with lamb.

2 cups cherry tomatoes
2 cups mushroom caps

Skewer, alternating tomatoes and mushrooms. Barbecue lamb skewers over grill for 10 minutes. Add tomato skewers and grill all 5 more minutes. Baste all skewers with marinade occasionally.

Serves 6

TACOS OR TOSTADAS

1   **pound lean ground beef**
1   **medium onion, minced**
1   **clove garlic, minced**
2   **tablespoons oil**

Sauté until meat is cooked. Drain.

1   **cup tomato sauce**
2   **teaspoons chili powder**
¼   **teaspoon cumin**
    Salt and pepper to taste

Add and simmer 20 minutes. Spoon into serving dish.

4   **cups cooked pinto beans, mashed**
¼   **cup bacon grease**
6   **green onions, minced**
8   **ounces Monterey Jack cheese, grated**

Combine and heat over low fire. Spoon into a serving dish.

Chopped onions
Diced tomatoes
Shredded lettuce
Shredded cabbage
Shredded carrots
Shredded cheese
Diced cucumbers

Arrange any combination of the vegetables and cheese on a platter.

12–16 corn tortillas

Fry each tortilla in hot oil about 3 minutes. Drain.

Tomato salsa (p. 431)
Sour cream

Have each person assemble his own tacos, layering shell, beans, meat, vegetables, and cheese. Drizzle with sauce and top with sour cream.

Serves 6

TEMPURA

Oil for deep frying

1 egg
1 cup water

Beat together.

1¹/₈ cups flour

Add, stirring 2 or 3 times to blend. A few lumps are fine.

¹/₄ cup soy sauce
¹/₂ cup dashi
2 teaspoons sugar

Mix and place sauce in serving bowl.

Radishes, grated
Ginger root, grated
Horseradish, grated

Place these condiments in separate bowls.

Snap beans, cut in 2-inch pieces
Eggplant, peeled and cut into fingers
Carrots, parboiled and diagonally
  sliced
Parsley
Summer squash, cut in fingers
Turnips, peeled and sliced
Green onions, sliced in 2-inch pieces
Large raw prawns, deveined and
  shelled (leave tail fins on)

Dry thoroughly, and dip in batter. Deep-fry in hot oil. When bubbles become small, the tempura is done. Drain and serve with soy sauce and condiments.

Serves 4–8

The secret of a good tempura is a light batter. An overmixed batter will result in heavy and excessively crusty tempura. Bowls of steaming rice should accompany tempura.

BEEF SUKIYAKI

4 ounces beef suet, quartered

Melt suet in a large electric frying pan at table.

$^1/_2$ **cup soy sauce**
$^1/_4$ **cup sake**
$^1/_3$ **cup sugar**

Mix together in a bowl to make sauce.

2 pounds beef tenderloin, thinly sliced

Each diner dips slices of meat into the sauce, then cooks it in the pan until a third of the meat has been used. Pour in sauce to cover pan and add rest of beef, cooking only until light brown.

2 cups shredded spinach
$^1/_2$ **cup Chinese cabbage, cut in fingers**
12 green onions, cut in 2-inch lengths
12 mushroom caps
1$^1/_2$ cups broccoli flowerets
12 cubes tofu, each 1 inch

Place atop beef. Cook 2 to 3 minutes and then transfer beef to the top. Cook over medium heat until vegetables are tender.

$^1/_4$ **cup dry mustard mixed with**
      2 tablespoons water
   Soy sauce
   Beaten raw egg
   Hot cooked rice

Divide into separate bowls for each diner, who removes cooked food with chopsticks, dips in mustard, soy sauce, or beaten egg, and eats with rice.

Serves 8

ASSYRIAN DOLMA

½ **cup butter**
2 **cups cooked diced lamb**
1 **chopped onion**

Sauté.

1 **cup uncooked rice**
1 **teaspoon salt**
1 **teaspoon paprika**
1 **cup minced green onions**
½ **cup minced celery**
½ **cup chopped fresh basil**
1 **cup chopped fresh parsley**

Combine with lamb.

6 **tomatoes**
4 **green peppers**
2 **8-inch summer squash, halved**

Hollow all vegetables, reserving tomato pulp. Turn upside down and drain. Stuff with lamb filling. Arrange in a baking dish.

2 **cups tomato sauce**
¼ **cup lemon juice**
½ **cup sugar**

Mix with tomato pulp and pour over vegetables. Bake at 325° for 1½ hours.

Serves 5–6

STUFFED FRENCH ROLLS

  2 **large tomatoes, chopped**
  3 **green onions, minced**
 ½ **cup chopped green olives**
 ¼ **cup chopped green pepper**
  1 **teaspoon vinegar**
  8 **ounces cheddar cheese, grated**
2–3 **tablespoons mayonnaise (optional)**

Mix and chill 2 to 24 hours.

  6 **French rolls**

Cut a hole in one end of roll and scoop out bread. Stuff with vegetable filling and bake at 350° for 30 minutes.

Serves 6

SUMMER SURPRISE CASSEROLE

1 **large onion, sliced**
1 **eggplant, peeled and cubed**
1 **cup uncooked rice**
1 **green pepper, diced**
3 **summer squash, sliced**
3 **tomatoes, peeled and sliced**
   Salt and pepper

Layer in a large oiled casserole, seasoning each vegetable layer.

1½ **cups beef consommé**
3   **tablespoons olive oil**

Mix and pour over top. Bake at 350° for 30 minutes covered, then uncovered for 15 minutes or until liquid is absorbed.

Serves 6

The perfect medley of flavors for a summer barbecue of beef or chicken. Here is rice and vegetables all in one.

VEGETABLE CHUTNEY

2 carrots, cut in 1-inch strips
1½ cups broken cauliflower
1 green pepper, diced
2 stalks celery, diagonally sliced
1 zucchini, diced
1 small red onion, sliced and
   separated into rings
¾ cup grape jelly
¾ cup vinegar
1 teaspoon fresh minced ginger
½ teaspoon dry mustard
½ teaspoon salt

Combine all in large kettle and heat to boiling. Ladle into hot sterilized jars and seal. Process in boiling water 10 minutes. Better after flavors have blended a few weeks.

4 pints

INDEX

491